CONSUMING KATRINA

for Elinor, with love,
Kate P. Hains

Folklore Studies in a Multicultural World

The Folklore Studies in a Multicultural World series is a collaborative venture of
the University of Illinois Press, the University Press of Mississippi, the University of
Wisconsin Press, and the American Folklore Society, made possible by a generous grant
from the Andrew W. Mellon Foundation. The series emphasizes the interdisciplinary
and international nature of current folklore scholarship, documenting connections
between communities and their cultural production. Series volumes highlight aspects of
folklore studies such as world folk cultures, folk art and music, foodways, dance, African
American and ethnic studies, gender and queer studies, and popular culture.

FOLKLORE STUDIES
IN A MULTICULTURAL
WORLD

CONSUMING KATRINA

Public Disaster and Personal Narrative

Kate Parker Horigan

University Press of Mississippi / Jackson

www.upress.state.ms.us

The University Press of Mississippi is a member
of the Association of American University Presses.

First printing 2018

∞

Library of Congress Cataloging-in-Publication Data

Names: Horigan, Kate Parker, author.
Title: Consuming Katrina: public disaster and
personal narrative / Kate Parker Horigan.
Description: Jackson : University Press of Mississippi, [2018] |
Includes bibliographical references and index. |
Identifiers: LCCN 2018000780 (print) | LCCN 2018012639 (ebook) |
ISBN 9781496817891 (epub single) | ISBN 9781496817907 (epub institutional) |
| ISBN 9781496817914 (pdf single) | ISBN 9781496817921 (pdf institutional) |
ISBN 9781496817884 (cloth : alk. paper)
Subjects: LCSH: Hurricane Katrina, 2005—Personal narratives. | Hurricane
Katrina, 2005—Social aspects—Louisiana—New Orleans. | Disaster victims—
Louisiana—New Orleans. | Disaster relief—Social aspects—United States. |
Disasters—Mississippi—Gulf Coast. | Refugees—Social aspects—Louisiana—
New Orleans. | New Orleans (La.)—Social conditions—21st century.
Classification: LCC HV636 2005 .L8 (ebook) | LCC HV636 2005 .L8 H67 2018
(print) | DDC 363.34/92280976335—dc23 LC record available at
https://lccn.loc.gov/2018000780

British Library Cataloging-in-Publication Data available

For the Katrina survivors who shared their stories
and for the people who made Louisiana home for me

CONTENTS

ACKNOWLEDGMENTS

Someone once told me that looking at the acknowledgments in books exposes the lie that writing is a solitary act. This book was certainly not created in solitude, and I owe thanks to all of those who made it possible and kept me company in one way or another.

The earliest seed of this project was planted in a literature seminar with Molly Travis at Tulane University, in the first semester following Hurricane Katrina. Even before that, though, I must thank the Department of English and Comparative Literature at Columbia University, who took me in during the "Katrina semester," when I might not have otherwise continued my studies.

At Ohio State, Amy Shuman was a champion of this research from the beginning, and she has continued to be a profound influence in my intellectual and personal life. My thanks also to Ray Cashman, Wendy Hesford, and Maurice Stevens for their help in shaping earlier versions of this book. I received support from the English Department and the Center for Folklore Studies at OSU and found incredible resources and communities there. Thanks especially to Elizabeth Bell, Katie Carmichael, Brad Freeman, Ryan Friedman, Alejandro Jacky, Anne Jansen, Meg LeMay, Barbara Lloyd, Brandon Manning, Corinne Martin, Brian McAllister, Dave McLaughlin, Galey Modan, Dorothy Noyes, Cassie Patterson, RaShelle Peck, Jim Phelan, Joe Ponce, and Catherine Sundt Vieira. The Writing in Depth Academic Writing Retreat, hosted by Maurice Stevens and Michelle Rivera-Clonch at Hope Springs Institute in Ohio, provided the physical and mental space to make writing progress at critical junctures.

Dorothy Noyes introduced me to Carl Lindahl, who introduced me to Pat Jasper, Shari Smothers, and the Surviving Katrina and Rita in Houston Project, which led me to the central claims of this book. Carl Lindahl's input and support have been invaluable through every step of this project, and his work with survivors continues to inspire me and teach me that there is much more to be done. I am indebted to all the participants of the SKRH interview project; moreover, I am thankful to all survivors who were willing to share their stories with me for the purpose of this research, including those at the

Delgado Storytelling Workshop, which would not have happened without Cathy Cooney Davis, Melanie Deffendall, Lica Gamble, and Matt Palumbo.

I am grateful to the colleagues I worked with as a lecturer at Indiana University, in the Department of Folklore and Ethnomusicology, especially for feedback on parts of this work offered by Henry Glassie, Diane Goldstein, John McDowell, and Pravina Shukla. Thanks also to Jesse Fivecoate and Maria Trogolo for their insights in our small but mighty seminar on folklore and disaster.

At Western Kentucky, I continue to be surrounded by supportive and inspiring colleagues. My thanks especially go to Erika Brady, Ann Ferrell, and Michael Ann Williams for their input. Potter College of Arts and Letters provided me with professional development funding that enabled research in New Orleans. I also appreciate the feedback offered by the Potter College Writing Group. Rachel Haberman provided essential research and editing assistance, all while finishing her master's in folk studies and having a baby girl.

Six months after having my own baby girl, when I could not imagine writing a coherent sentence, much less finishing a book, I received notice that the University Press of Mississippi had selected my book proposal for the Folklore Studies in a Multicultural World author workshop. That workshop, supported by the Andrew W. Mellon Foundation and the American Folklore Society, launched me into the final stages of manuscript preparation. All of the author, mentor, and editor participants provided helpful feedback, especially my workshop mentor, Jay Mechling, and my first editor, Craig Gill. I have since had the pleasure of working with Katie Keene, Mary Heath, and others at the press, and I appreciate their guidance. I am also indebted to my copyeditor, Camille Hale, and to the two anonymous reviewers for their time and their extremely helpful insights.

Along the way, I have also sought and received excellent advice from Carrie Gillogly, Spencer Parker, Cynthia Kimball, and—at pretty much every point—Sheila Bock. Finally, I am always filled with loving gratitude when I think of my immediate and extended family: my parents, Craig and Betsy Parker; my in-laws John and Debbie Horigan; my siblings/siblings-in-law and their spouses and children; and, especially, my husband, Patrick, and our daughter, Grace.

An earlier version of chapter 2 appeared in *Mapping Generations of Traumatic Memory in American Narratives*, edited by Dana Mihăilescu and Roxana Oltean (Newcastle: Cambridge Scholars Publishing, 2014). An earlier version of chapter 3 was published in *Ten Years after Katrina*, edited by Mary Ruth Marotte and Glenn Jellenik (Lanham: Lexington Books, 2015).

CONSUMING KATRINA

INTRODUCTION

In August 2005, I drove out of New Orleans in the middle of the night, headed for I-59 in a rattling, red truck. We sat three across the single bench seat—me, my roommate, and her boyfriend—with a large dog squeezed in at our feet. Hitched to the truck was the boyfriend's old boat; in the boat was a wooden crate; and in the crate were six chickens we had been raising in our backyard. Whenever I think about my Hurricane Katrina story, I remember the chickens: towing birds in a boat on a highway was bizarre. Just before the hurricane landed in Louisiana, we arrived in Nashville, where we slept on a friend's floor. We watched every news broadcast; we called everyone we had left behind; we listened first to reports from friends and then later to automated messages telling us the numbers were not available. As the news got unimaginably worse, we cried, we tried to sleep, and we watched more. We searched the web for images of our apartment on Freret Street. We waited. Six weeks later, we knew our place was flooded; eight weeks later we went in to drag what we could from our mold-infested rooms. The mold sent my roommate to the hospital with toxicosis and left me with an olfactory memory like a noxious version of Proust's madeleines. We moved into a new apartment and settled into our strange post-Katrina lives in New Orleans. Years later, I still think about that smell and those chickens.

In October 2009, I sat in an airport bar in Chicago, en route to a meeting of the American Folklore Society, and stared in stunned silence at the stranger next to me as she proclaimed that people in New Orleans had a "victim mentality," and anyone who had not evacuated or did not possess the "gumption" to rebuild on their own was "too stupid to live." First, I thought about sharing with her my own story, all the nuances of evacuation: how I had not wanted to leave but had been persuaded to at the last minute; how the truck needed a jump start, and we almost changed our minds because of that; and how I depended on resources from family and friends outside the city in order to leave. Or I could have attempted to explain the enormous obstacles to rebuilding—financial, physical, social, emotional—including the fundamental fear that the city was not safe. I wanted to convince her she was wrong in believing in an image of Katrina survivors as helpless and dependent victims, but eventually I ended up walking away, leaving her midsentence, my silent departure the only protest I could muster. I still think about that woman, too, and about the things I could have said to her that might have changed her mind.

There are no ready answers for people who ask you to explain yourself or your city in the aftermath of an event like Katrina, which was, according to the federal government, "the single most catastrophic natural disaster in U.S. history."[1] But there are better ways to frame our questions and contextualize our stories: ways to elicit the kinds of personal narratives that Katrina survivors shared in the Surviving Katrina and Rita in Houston project (SKRH),[2] in interviews that were the catalyst for this book. Reframing the way we talk about disaster allows us to recognize the strategies that survivors employ as they reconstruct and reflect on what they have endured. For many of the interviewees in SKRH, this means narrating the tragedies they witnessed in a way that foregrounds their own compassion and competence in the face of neglect and chaos. For other survivors discussed in the following chapters, they emphasize ambiguity, distance themselves from stereotypical categories, share their awareness about how stories such as theirs might be circulated and received, and protest official modes of remembering Katrina. Paying attention to these rhetorical strategies affords survivors the audience they deserve, and it also paves the way for implementing their own theories about how to cope and rebuild. Survivors are the experts on their own experiences, and as such, the greatest resource for recovery.[3]

After I returned to New Orleans in 2005, I found myself surrounded by people telling the same stories again and again. They were obsessed with Katrina, with describing how they suffered and prevailed. I noticed this in my everyday conversations and in local culture. I saw it in the classes I took, as a graduate student at Tulane University, and later in the writing courses I taught at Delgado Community College. Those narrative responses were in part a show of resistance: New Orleanians were not satisfied with the story as it was being circulated in the national discourse, so, privately, among ourselves, as we went back to work and school, we kept repeating, "This is how it really happened to me." I also had been telling everyone I knew about the chickens, the mold—it was outrageous; it was painful; we kept our sense of humor; we made it. But that is not the kind of story that fits easily into a conversation in the Chicago airport.

Nor are the complex and powerful stories shared in SKRH interviews the kind of stories that get snapped up by publishers, or broadcast on the news, made to represent the generalized experiences of Katrina survivors. The kinds of stories that are easy to share, and that do get widely circulated and remembered, are those that confirm the expectations of a broad national audience: books like *Zeitoun* and *A.D.: New Orleans after the Deluge*, documentaries like *Trouble the Water*; texts featuring caricatures of heroism, anger, resilience. These are not the complicated narrations wherein survivors enact strategies that advance their own recovery and that ought to inform the formation of public memorials and long-term recovery plans. Rather, they are stories that bear the appearance of the particular—thereby increasing their cultural capital among audiences eager to consume authentic experiences of suffering—but actually reflect dominant narratives about race, class, religion, gender, region, and human response to trauma. Stories such as these propagate dangerously limited and stereotypical representations, which in turn inform responses to disasters such as Katrina. They also allow audiences to feel sympathy for survivors, without feeling complicit in their conditions of suffering or compelled to act. There is, however, great potential for an alternative to such representations, and it already exists in nascent forms, drawn out in the chapters that follow: narrators negotiate the ways their stories are shared, and those negotiations can be incorporated into the stories themselves as they travel beyond communities of survivors. When trauma becomes public, as the insatiable appetite for disaster stories demands that it must, the texts that most ethically adapt personal narratives are those that include survivors' own critical engagement with processes of narrative production.

Personal Narrative and Public Disaster

Major disasters attract the public eye for a complicated array of reasons: empathy for victims, modern media spectacles of suffering, the aesthetic and philosophical appeal of ruins, the political theater that often follows, and our attendant fears about environmental precarity. In recent decades, the attention disasters receive exemplifies another trend, that of interest in the vernacular. Diane Goldstein points out that "the move away from dominant narratives to individual narratives in postmodern culture has elevated the role of storytellers, witnesses, testimony, life story, and personal experience narrative in all aspects of public culture around us" (2015:127). Narratives of massive disaster are incomprehensible in their scale, so in their place we encounter individual narratives of personal experience: the eyewitnesses to catastrophe.[4] Although Goldstein advises that "actual awareness and accountability" can accompany attention to vernacular knowledge and narrative, she also warns of those who are "achieving visual credit through manipulation of interest in the vernacular" (2015:127). It is this sort of manipulation that more often than not characterizes representations of Hurricane Katrina and other large-scale disasters. When personal narratives are presented as representative of disaster-affected communities, they shape how those communities are seen. As personal narratives are attached to larger dominant discourses, they influence public perception and memory of disaster, and also response and recovery, generally in negative ways. Though this is a disturbing trend, it is also a hopeful site for intervention: folklorists and others who are experts in the circulation of personal narratives can apply their knowledge to observe how individuals are talking about their experiences and to incorporate diverse vernacular responses in the narration, memorialization, and recovery efforts that follow disasters.

To date, scholars have done a great deal to bring attention to patterns in news media representations of Katrina.[5] Most germane to the current study, media representations fell into stereotypes similar to those that populate later published works: "[E]ven while engaging extensively in both reporting and public service, the media also presented highly oversimplified and distorted characterizations of the human response to the Katrina catastrophe" (Tierney, Bevc, and Kuligowski 2006:73). Folklorists have studied aspects of vernacular and official responses to Katrina, including cultural traditions threatened by the hurricane (Abrahams 2006), the legends that proliferated after the storm (Lindahl 2012b; see also de Caro 2013), and the emergence of new rhetorical phenomena in post-Katrina contexts (Gipson 2014; Noyes 2016).[6] This scholarship helps situate my investigation into personal narratives about Katrina, as they have been adapted, publicly circulated, and projected onto the long-term memory of the event. More immediately relevant, however, are current understandings of the complex relationships between narrative, memory, and trauma on a public scale.

Narrators of disaster and other story-worthy events face a crisis in credibility (Labov 1982). They attempt to relate the extraordinary nature of their experience, while at the same time they rely on ordinary narrative conventions (Shuman 2005). When personal narratives of disaster are made public, audiences expect both reportability and credibility, creating a complex set of demands for narrators and publishers alike. Credibility is also subject to cultural expectations based on other prevailing narratives: "[t]he story that is too unfamiliar, too exotic to be believed, and the story that is too familiar are both subject to suspicion" (Shuman 2005:54). Thus, in constructing a story that makes a bid for an audience and for believability, the teller must strike the perfect balance of exceptionality and familiarity. This balance is further complicated by the social aspects of narrative and of disaster.

Despite their name, personal narratives are inherently social in their creation, their transmission, and their function. Like life stories, personal experience narratives respond to a social need for coherence and follow shared scripts (Linde 1993; see also Titon 1980; Olney 1984; Portelli 1991; Tonkin 1992). As in contexts of illness, where dominant cultural narratives follow a trajectory that personal experience is expected to mimic (Frank 1995), there are predetermined narratives that characterize disaster. As Arthur Frank puts it, "people do not make up their stories by themselves. The shape of the telling is molded by all the rhetorical expectations that the storyteller has been internalizing" (3). Social expectations influence the creation of stories, then, and social relationships also provide the means for making sense of experiences.

When a community is disrupted as in contexts of disaster, individuals lose access to multiple narrative resources: their sense of self, their connection to a group identity, even the material conditions in which their stories are usually told (Tonkin 1992; see also Myerhoff 1992; Cashman 2008). Individuals are still expected to produce coherent narratives, however, and the stakes are heightened in contexts of trauma (Goodall and Lee 2015:8–9). External audiences—such as media outlets, government or other aid agencies, and even strangers—continue to demand a story that makes sense. Narrative coherence garners real rewards for those who manage to convey it, and for those whom it eludes, the negative consequences are just as real.[7] If the rhetorical resources to which individuals turn to construct coherent narratives are not available, then the stories they create will suffer: "Many stories and histories simply cannot be told when the social frameworks are not there" (Plummer 2001:402). As a result, coherence is sometimes imposed on complex narratives by others, as in the case studies that follow, to the detriment of the narrators and their ruptured communities. Thus, under the guise of a survivor's personal narrative, dominant narratives of disaster are delivered to eager audiences.

Dominant narratives frequently become the bases for public memory of disasters, as is the case with "resilience" in the memorialization of Katrina (discussed in chapter 5). Recent scholarship, building on early to mid-twentieth-century work, explores collective aspects of remembering large-scale events. Early views of collective memory, such as those proposed by Maurice Halbwachs (1992), were relatively static, casting people as passive vessels and failing to account for the capacity of individuals to modify memory (Tonkin 1992).[8] Later models have become increasingly dynamic; for example, historian Guy Beiner distinguishes between what constitutes memory as opposed to the actions of remembering, electing to use "the term *social memory* when referring to representations of traditional bodies of knowledge, and *social remembering* (or simply *remembrance*) in reference to dynamic processes of reproduction" (Beiner 2007:28).[9] As Beiner argues and as the chapters that follow illustrate, "it is possible to positively identify . . . moments of social remembering in action" (28). Social remembering happens in part via the production, circulation, and reception of personal narratives. This circulation is not one-directional; not only do personal narratives shape public memory of large-scale events, but those public expressions also feed back into personal recollections of experience.[10]

Despite their utility, Beiner's categories have not really taken hold, and scholars continue to use "collective" and "social" memory, as well as "public" memory.[11] Goodall and Lee differentiate usefully among terms by claiming that "[c]ollective memory occurs when individuals separately remember the same event," whereas "public memory forms when a people remember in and through inter-subjective relationships with other members of the public" (2015:4–5). Others emphasize this interactive quality as well. In their study of a flooded Australian community, Madsen and O'Mullan write that "while social memories can be associated with historical and cultural artefacts such as memorials," it is also important to focus on "the communication that occurs between individuals and throughout communities that creates narratives and ways of interpreting events such as natural disasters" (2013:60). The following chapters venture into analysis of these social relationships and communications.

The public memory of disaster is enacted in works of art and literature, museums and monuments, special celebrations, and everyday life.[12] In New Orleans, as in other disaster-affected areas,

> the re-telling of stories is as influential as living the experiences. That is, the sto-
> ries told around the kitchen table, over a beer at the pub, as well as the portrayals
> of experiences via television news reports, documentaries, and online lay the
> foundations for social memories that will be drawn on in the future and that will
> influence how that community responds to future adverse events. (Madsen and
> O'Mullan 2013:68)

The personal narratives that describe Katrina in public contexts shape how it is remembered. As the memorialization of Katrina in monuments and anniversary celebrations reveals, the themes of those narratives get taken up in published texts and in material and customary culture. This study of Katrina looks at expressions of memory and at how memories take shape, circulate, and gain force in social contexts.

One of Katrina's most complex social contexts is that of shared traumatic experience. The notion of what trauma is and who is a victim of it is complex and historically contingent, and only in recent decades have comprehensive theories of collective or social trauma emerged.[13] Despite shifts in how trauma has been understood over time, the popular tendency to see "trauma" and "victim" as stable categories can prevent nuanced understanding of the conditions that create suffering (Young 1995; Fassin and Rechtman 2009; Stevens 2009). With respect to Hurricane Katrina, "the people of New Orleans were already victims of poverty and discrimination that reinforced class inequalities through racial distinctions. Trauma is not only silent on these realities; it actually obscures them" (Fassin and Rechtman 2009:281). Likewise, public perception of what makes someone a "legitimate victim" of trauma influences how personal stories of disaster are adapted, often in ways that obscure the lived realities of survivors.

Published accounts of disasters such as Katrina depict individuals as exemplary of massive suffering but also as disconnected from the social structures that produce it and the social networks that can mitigate it. Partly as a result of these representations, only survivors' most recent grievances are acknowledged and remediated, rather than those underlying structural issues that predate and predetermine the crisis. Furthermore, solutions to problems are conceived of in terms of individual redress, rather than communal rebuilding. In contrast to the customary explanation of trauma as a single overwhelming event, "trauma is ongoing and chronic when the social conditions that bring it about are chronic" (Pintar 2006:53). Sociologist Kai Erikson explains that "'trauma' has to be understood as resulting from a *constellation of life experiences* as well as from a discrete happening, from a *persisting condition* as well as from an acute event" (1994:229, emphasis in original).[15] Erikson concludes that communal trauma can take the form of "damage to the tissues that hold human groups intact" (237). A similar model describes social forces that enable trauma as a "machine in which a tie to others and to living are rendered impossible" (Biehl 2005:186). These metaphors suggest a need to investigate what exactly constitutes the connective "tissues" or "ties" in a particular social body—as well as their vulnerabilities as exposed by disaster. In personal experience narratives post-Katrina, the connections that community members lay claim to are different than the individualism that becomes highlighted as their narratives travel to wide audiences (Bock and Horigan 2015). Recognizing and reinstating such ties is crucial to disaster recovery.

Traumatic experiences during disaster are social because of how they are collectively felt and remembered, but also because of the social nature of experience itself:

> Subjects are constituted discursively and experience is a linguistic event (it doesn't happen outside established meanings), but neither is it confined to a fixed

order of meaning. Since discourse is by definition shared, experience is collective as well as individual. (Scott 1991:793)[16]

Personal narratives reflect this discourse that "is by definition shared"; they reveal the complex, collective aspects of experience, and they illuminate the processes of social remembrance. When personal narratives are stripped of the social, dynamic contexts that create them, though, they become misrepresentations of experience. Those narratives that reach public audiences and manage to carry along the messy complexities of their social roots are those that bear true potential for a recovery that is also aware and inclusive of the social body.

Ernst van Alphen writes, regarding traumatic experience, "[T]he problem is not the nature of the event, nor an intrinsic limitation of representation; rather, it is the split between the living of an event and the available forms of representation with/in which the event can be experienced" (1999:27). Van Alphen differentiates himself from those who see trauma as a failure of mental integration, whereas he sees the issue as a linguistic or narrative one. Van Alphen emphasizes that if the preexisting language that will make sense of an experience does not exist, that does not mean the experience is not "real" in some sense, but rather that the experience is impossible to make sense of. He argues that this is a semiotic problem rather than a psychological one and that it can be addressed by using modes of discourse other than the historical mode: "[I]f the problem originates in a technical discursive limitation, the realm of the imaginative might be a solution . . . and even provide some privileged access, as it pursues its role of creatively challenging the symbolic order" (van Alphen 1997:42). He explains how he sees these imaginative discourses as capable of representing the "unrepresentable":

> History brings with it more responsibilities than only knowing and remembering the facts . . . Other responsibilities that are poignantly imposed on us involve the working through of the traumatic intrusion of an unimaginable reality, and the foregrounding of the cracks and tears that are concealed by the coherence of the stories being told. It is in relation to those responsibilities that the imaginative discourses of art and literature can step in. (van Alphen 1997:37)

For the ethical representation of traumatic experience, "foregrounding . . . the cracks and tears" is essential. Although van Alphen favors imaginative fictional works, there are places where creative nonfiction texts successfully do this, as subsequent chapters will show. In fact, "cracks and tears" can surface not only in a text, revealing discrepancies between an incoherent experience and a coherent narrative, but also in the processes by which that narrative is translated from personal to public, in its articulation of the ties that bind social bodies. These ruptures ought to be featured, rather than fixed, in the texts that publicize personal experience of disaster.

Just as Goodall and Lee define public memory as that which occurs "when a people remember in and through inter-subjective relationships with other members of the public," we might conceptualize of a "public disaster" as something more than just an instance of multiple people experiencing the same event. A public disaster is one in which survivors experience traumatic events within the context of social relationships and that also causes harm to those relationships. This idea of "public" extends beyond the communities directly affected by disasters, to those broader audiences who hear stories about the events (and for whom, in many cases, those stories are crafted). The public aspect of disasters is also demonstrated in the rhetoric surrounding their memorialization. In what follows, I apply a model that takes these public dynamics of disasters into account and, consequently, suggests a more ethical approach to circulating the personal narratives that describe them.

Analyzing Interactive Contexts

The narratives that emerge from disaster derive meaning within contexts of social interaction. My study, therefore, attends to various performances and interpretations within such contexts, as personal narratives about Katrina are produced, circulated, and received.[17] In oral narratives from SKRH interviews, for example, I emphasize the rhetorical strategies of narrators, rather than the content of their narration. But interactive context extends beyond the immediate situation of a face-to-face conversation. When Dell Hymes applies his "ethnography of communication," he includes "all elements that constitute the communicative economy of a group" (1974:4). This extends to aspects of context such as the "knowledge and insight" of community members (8), which is especially instructive in the case of Katrina, as survivors interpret how their narratives are circulated and received within and beyond their communities.

The contexts in which narratives are shared are not preexisting ones, but rather ones that are constituted by the interactions themselves as texts are constructed and performed (Duranti and Goodwin 1992). The process by which context emerges in performance has been termed "contextualization" (Briggs 1988:15). In personal narratives about Hurricane Katrina, narrators engage in sometimes subtle and sometimes blatant attempts to shape the contexts of their story's production, circulation, and reception. Unlike those "[m]any analysts [who] have . . . found it both fruitful and unproblematic to devote their energies to description and analysis of the internal structure of stories while ignoring the interaction through which they were in fact told in the first place" (Duranti and Goodwin 11), I argue for critical attention to these interactions and, furthermore, for inclusion of these interactions into publications that distribute the resulting stories.

Studying "the interactional activity through which narratives are constructed, communicated, and sustained or reconfigured" requires attention to the contexts in which those interactions occur (Gubrium and Holstein 2009:xvii). It also demands investigation into the power dynamics of various contextual influences on those narratives. In the case of disaster stories, the interplay of personal narratives and dominant cultural ones is multidirectional, but the effects these narratives have on each other are not equivalent. Dominant discourses tend to absorb or appropriate the particularities of survivors' stories, with the result of making them familiar to audiences, but also of upholding the interests of powerful groups by reifying those narratives that bestow power on them. Following Gubrium and Holstein, then, I ask not only "how the leading 'big stories' of various settings relate to the individual 'little stories' that participants communicate within them" (2009:124), but also attempt to "demonstrat[e] ethnographically how cultural or organizational resources and preferences are brought to bear in the interactional production or preclusion of particular narratives" (2009:52). I do this by combining analysis of micro- and macrolevels of discourse relating to Hurricane Katrina.[18]

Contextualization cues in the texts determine the elements of interactive context on which I focus. The contexts that are relevant to a particular narrative are those that are indexed by the narrative itself, and they may be distal, proximal, or both. Holstein and Gubrium explain that context is "construed in terms of 'distal' factors such as culture, socio-economic status, or social structure, or more 'proximal' conditions such as interactional settings or sequences" (2004:298). Such broad definitions of context have the potential to be unwieldy; as Briggs puts it, "[t]he task of describing the context thus takes on the form of an infinite regress" (1988:13). Ray Cashman's method for deciding what is "relevant context" helps to address this issue: "I prefer to begin with proximal aspects of situational context as it unfolds moment-by-moment, but then, when needed, I shift to distal aspects of context. . . . Such broader issues require comment, particularly when narrators reference them in the process of contextualizing their stories" (2012:187). Likewise, in my study of Katrina survivors' personal narratives, which comprises a variety of discursive domains, I attempt to keep my focus on the most salient features of text, process, and context. As I draw comparisons among narratives of Katrina survivors; among the processes through which they are produced, distributed, and consumed in mainstream publications and venues; and among their discursive contexts, the emphases and concerns of survivor-narrators take center stage—as they ought to in the texts that make their stories public.

Conclusion

My study begins, in chapter 1, with analysis of oral narratives shared in the interactive context of interviews for the SKRH project. In these complex and often dramatic exchanges, survivors interview one another about experiences during the hurricane. The speakers use rhetorical strategies that show their concern with telling a coherent story and explaining the consistency of their logic during Katrina's chaos. The interviewers and interviewees also demonstrate careful attention to their interactions with one another, and their exchanges become part of the textual products (recording and transcript) of the interview. Consequently, listeners can observe how the dialogue between participants enables interviewees to exhibit greater control over their own positioning as narrators. Finally, SKRH interviewees emphasize their personal responsibility as narrators in the interactional context of the interviews and as actors in the events they describe. This insistence evokes a dominant narrative of irresponsibility among Katrina's victims that, although it is not explicitly referred to by these survivors, is simultaneously conjured and interrupted by their protestations against it.

When I listened to and transcribed the interviews of SKRH participants, I noticed how participants in this project, on both sides of the microphone, negotiated the context of their communication in order to allow complex narratives to emerge. As I listened to interviewers and interviewees establishing relationships, finding common ground for communication, and sometimes challenging each other, I wondered whether these kinds of negotiations happen in contexts where survivors' personal stories are collected using ethnographic methods such as interviewing, but then adapted for wide mainstream distribution. I discovered that survivors do continue to negotiate the contexts of their storytelling, but in the processes of publishing, these negotiations tend to get edited out or obscured, rather than foregrounded within the stories themselves. The three nonfiction case studies herein were selected because of their popularity and because they are all based—like the SKRH project—on in-depth interviews with Katrina survivors. Therefore, it seemed reasonable to expect to encounter similar kinds of interaction around narrative production that exist in the SKRH collection. What I found, however, is that more often than not there is only the appearance of that interaction, carefully managed by the authors, publishers, and producers of these texts and made to look like consensus rather than conflict. In chapters 2, 3, and 4, I discuss these three texts and show how they reinforce dominant narratives related to disaster. I also describe the limited instances in which survivors manage to engage with and occasionally challenge their problematic representations.

In chapter 2, I discuss Abdulrahman Zeitoun's Katrina narrative, which has found great commercial success in its adaptation in *Zeitoun*, Dave Eggers's nonfiction bestseller. A version of this story was first shared as a public blog authored by Zeitoun himself, then an interview version was published both in Billy Sothern's *Down in New Orleans: Reflections from a Drowned City* (2007) and in *Voices from the Storm* (2006), edited by Lola Vollen and Chris Ying. Finally, an extended version as told by Dave Eggers was published in Eggers's 2009 book. Zeitoun's story reaches the peak of its circulation when it is told by someone else, an authority figure who vouches for the story's credibility but also promises readers that it is still Zeitoun's personal narrative, the events of Katrina seen "through his eyes" (Eggers 2009b:345). The changes in Zeitoun's story from blog to book, however, reflect a narrative transition from an urgent first-person account laden with ambiguity, to a lyrical drama that offers clear resolution. Ultimately, Dave Eggers presents Zeitoun as a folk hero—an immigrant turned self-made businessman who, when disaster strikes, steps up to battle natural forces and rescue helpless women. When Zeitoun is unjustly incarcerated in Katrina's wake, readers can feel self-righteously outraged at the villains of Islamophobia and the prison-industrial complex. Both the figure of Zeitoun and the public response to him, though, are complicated by later criminal charges against him of domestic assault. Despite Abdulrahman's early involvement in narrating his story himself in his blog and interviews, when it comes to the bestselling book *Zeitoun*, the survivor's engagement with the narration is absent, and the result is a dangerously one-sided picture of a complex individual.

Chapter 3 describes another example of a popular publication based on the narratives of real Katrina survivors: the nonfiction graphic novel *A.D.: New Orleans after the Deluge*, by comic artist Josh Neufeld. The print version of this book was published in 2009, but before that, it was released as a webcomic. In both versions of *A.D.*, the rhetorical and artistic choices of the author, in part influenced by the medium of comics and in part by publishers' demands, reinforce stereotypical categorizations, especially of African Americans. The interactive contexts that are particularly interesting in the case of *A.D.* are the characters' comments on Neufeld's representations of them in the webcomic. These conversations are similar to the SKRH interviews, where survivors negotiate the terms of their stories' production. Because the webcomic is serial and public, audiences are privy to this dialogue, meaning narrators' negotiations are built into the circulation and reception of the textual product, as they are in SKRH. However, despite his interest in fair representation, Neufeld publishes the print version without the web commentary. This chapter raises questions like those posed by Charles Briggs: "Why do some narratives become authoritative? Why are statements that challenge them erased from public discourse?" (2005:272). In the case of *A.D.*, we see Katrina survivors' challenging statements erased from the eventual print publication of the text.

Chapter 4 examines a final nonfiction, Katrina-based text with wide circulation, Tia Lessin and Carl Deal's 2008 documentary *Trouble the Water*. The filmmakers use unique documentary techniques that incorporate—to some extent—narrators' engagement with the processes of their story's publication. Specifically, the film includes survivor Kim Roberts's own footage, shot during Katrina on her handheld camera. Kim's role as documentarian is foregrounded, and in some striking scenes she expresses her awareness about the value of her story and its likelihood of circulating among particular kinds of audiences. Such scenes prevent the reception of these stories as mere confirmation of what audiences already believe. By incorporating Kim's assessment of the consumption that she knows her story is likely to encounter, the filmmakers successfully integrate survivors' own critiques of the discourses that typically represent them, and in the process, disrupt the easy empathy that often accompanies reception of personal narratives associated with trauma. However, the film's optimistic conclusion evokes a dominant narrative of individualistic uplift, a neoliberal twist that undermines the powerful work the film is otherwise performing.

Chapter 5 focuses on material and customary responses to Katrina and examines how those also tend to oversimplify complex narratives of suffering and recovery. Specifically, I reflect on ethnographic fieldwork conducted during the tenth anniversary of Katrina (in 2015) and observe how memorials, commemorative events, and everyday activities express multiple modes of remembering Katrina. This multiplicity was not exhibited in official discourse regarding the tenth anniversary, which stuck with a single campaign message of "Resilient New Orleans." Vernacular memorialization illustrates the same basic concept evident in previous chapters: people affected by disaster are already engaged in negotiating how that disaster gets remembered, and it is important to listen to those negotiations and not erase them from public representations and discourse.

In my concluding chapter, I review how these "recontextualizations" (Briggs 2005:273) of Katrina survivors' personal narratives reveal the dialogic nature of personal narratives made public, and I explore potential applications for my framework for understanding public disaster. Those narratives that find commercial success, broad distribution, and a place in official memorialization are those that uphold dominant narratives and let audiences off the hook in terms of an ethical obligation to the survivors whose stories they consume. The stories actually being told by survivors—even in the very publications and venues that reinforce prevalent misconceptions—are in fact much more complex than they often appear. After witnessing, myself, the frustration of trying to find the right context for sharing Katrina stories, and struggling to tell the right stories for the contexts we find ourselves in; after hearing the complexity in the content of the SKRH interviews and the negotiations which produced them, I was driven to question how interactive contexts and stories of disaster mutually constitute each other. When trauma is public, as in disasters like Katrina, personal narratives are often the means by which we understand and remember it. Texts conveying the eyewitness accounts of survivors have an obligation to include narrators' critical engagement with the processes by which their stories are being collected and shared. Ultimately, survivors' challenges to their own generalized representations should be incorporated into the discourses of disaster, especially because, as the case of Katrina has demonstrated, those discourses have a great deal to do with response, memory, and recovery.

CHAPTER ONE

"Establish Some Kind of Control": Survivor Interviews

I n the aftermath of Hurricane Katrina, during which Texans saw an influx of hundreds of thousands of evacuees, folklorists Carl Lindahl and Pat Jasper orchestrated the Surviving Katrina and Rita in Houston project (SKRH). The organizers describe the project as follows:

> [This collection of oral histories is] the first large-scale project in which the survivors of a major disaster have taken the lead in documenting it. The survivors received training and compensation to record fellow survivors' stories of the storm, their memories of home, and their ongoing struggles to build new communities in exile. ("Surviving Katrina and Rita in Houston" 2010:37)[1]

In these interviews, survivors explain their impulse to articulate what they have been through: they mention the therapeutic effect of sharing a traumatic story with an empathetic audience; the belief that their experiences are meaningful to others as inspiration, cautionary tale, or historical record; and the desire to counteract negative portrayals of New Orleanians in the news media and other public discourse. Shawn and Patrice,[2] two African American survivors of Hurricane Katrina, were displaced from New Orleans and interviewed for SKRH. These narrators, like many of those in the forty interviews with which I worked,[3] employ rhetorical strategies that contend with dominant discourses, especially those about race and responsibility in the context of Katrina. Within these dramatic accounts, Shawn and Patrice position themselves positively, contradicting widespread representations of African American survivors as either criminals or helpless victims and portraying themselves instead as competent and caring human beings.

In the case of SKRH, where the interviewers and interviewees are both hurricane survivors, the interactional context is not a traditional, information-gathering interview. Although in some oral history projects, interviewees are seen as information resources, folklorists in recent decades have largely followed Charles Briggs's contention regarding interviews that "context-sensitive features of such discourse are more clearly tied to the context of the interview than to that of the situation it describes" (1986:3). Thus, "interview results are as actively constructed, collaborative, and situationally mediated as other communicative ventures," and, consequently, "it is important to treat interviews as occasions for narrative work and not just information transfer" (Gubrium and Holstein 2009:7).

Folkloristic and sociolinguistic tools draw out the "text, texture, and context"[4] of these interview narratives:

> [L]inguistic analysis in an extended sense . . . cover[s] not only the traditional levels of analysis within linguistics (phonology, grammar up to the level of the sentence, and vocabulary and semantics) but also analysis of textual organization above the sentence, including intersentential cohesion and various aspects of the structure of texts which have been investigated by discourse analysts and conversation analysts (including properties of dialogue such as the organization of turn-taking). (Fairclough 1995:188)

This extended sense of linguistic analysis includes elements such as speaker transitions, framing, reported speech, collaboration, and variability in performance. Furthermore, these interviews might answer the following questions: "What sorts of practices are utilized to assemble and reflexively sustain narrative agency, authority, and competence? How do accountability and storytelling fit into the equation?" (Gubrium and Holstein 2009:160). In these oral interviews as well as in the published texts discussed in the following chapters, the contexts of production shape the narratives. A unique aspect of the interviews, though, is that the narrators' engagement with the processes of narrative production is heightened by virtue of the genre: the ways in which these survivors create and critique their communicative contexts is the inspiration for subsequent investigations, where the genres obscure rather than include those interactions. In all the texts examined here, there is room for further contextualization. The absence of personal information seems especially conspicuous in the discussion of survivor interviews; generally, folklorists work to provide a fuller picture of the narrators whose stories they share. However, this is precisely the problem of publicized narratives—all audiences know is what the text (in this case, the interview recording) tells them. Although further context would enrich understanding of the speakers discussed here, my analysis is limited to the contextualizing work that they do themselves: what they say is what you get.

Shawn and Patrice engage directly with their interlocutors, and they constitute larger discursive contexts for their stories by invoking and responding to dominant narratives regarding Katrina. The speakers implicitly bring these narratives into their accounts and refute them. Both Shawn and Patrice are notably concerned with discourses of responsibility, or more precisely, the prevailing perception that New Orleanians most injured by Katrina were to blame for their suffering by virtue of their personal irresponsibility. This view was circulated primarily with respect to the city's working-class African American population. In Shawn's case, this discourse surfaces as a characterization of both law enforcement officers and prisoners as irresponsible and criminal, a representation that Shawn rejects within his narrative. Patrice reacts to the depiction of Katrina's victims as passive and helpless and portrays instead her willingness to take responsibility for her family and fellow survivors.

"They Didn't Know What Was Really Going On": Shawn's Story

Shawn, a young sheriff's deputy, recalls the flooding of the Orleans Parish Prison. While reconstructing this event in narrative form, Shawn builds a credible image of himself acting responsibly despite the limited information available to him at the time of the storm. This self-representation contrasts dominant narratives portraying lower-level law enforcers as irresponsible, abandoning their posts as soon as the opportunity arose. A young woman named Amber interviews Shawn, who spent his twenty-eight years prior to Katrina living in the Upper Ninth Ward of New Orleans. From the start of this two-and-a-half-hour interview, there is substantial evidence of rapport, empathy, and shared communicative norms between Amber and Shawn, a discursive space of the sort that Shawn and other survivors have been denied in most representations of Katrina. These qualities create a favorable interactional context, and both collaborative and individual narratives emerge as a result.

The interview between Amber and Shawn begins on a friendly note; both participants are laughing and sounding at ease. The interviewer appears to already know some things about Shawn's life; for example, she prompts him— "you have sisters"—rather than asking an open-ended question about his family (Shawn 2008). Amber eventually reveals to her interviewee that she used to live in his neighborhood. Shawn calculates that her former address was about eight blocks from his, and he laughs while observing, "[W]e was close" (Shawn 2008). As Shawn begins recounting the days leading up to the hurricane, which he spent at his job as a deputy in Orleans Parish Prison, Amber interjects about every two minutes to ask for or offer more information: "And you were working at the—," "Saturday was two days before," "And how old is he?" "On your what?" "What do you mean, like—," and then finally, "Let me interrupt you for a second. Just so I can understand, so I can visualize. So the first floor—what's—is the first floor for the people that work there? Are there inmates there, or—?" (Shawn 2008). After this, as Shawn continues to talk, Amber's questions are more spread out and are limited to clarification, sometimes as simple as asking, "What?" As Gubrium and Holstein have noted, "At minimum, a conversation partner must refrain from speaking and pass on opportunities to speak at possible speakership transition points for an extended story to emerge" (2009:97–98). Because of Amber's increasingly withheld speech, at one point, Shawn talks for thirty uninterrupted minutes. An hour and forty minutes in, Amber asks the first question that is not an immediate response to a comment by Shawn. In this later portion of the interview, Amber asks general follow-up questions, inquiring about details from earlier in Shawn's narrative, or asking where the people from his story are now, and their talk becomes conversational, with a more even exchange.

This last section, which goes on for about forty minutes, also contains the thread of a play frame throughout, during which Shawn talks about getting himself a new house built in New Orleans by the television show *Extreme Makeover: Home Edition*, and Amber responds in joking encouragement. As Jennifer Coates explains this kind of linguistic event, "[t]he idea of talk as play draws on Bateson's (1953) idea of a play frame. Bateson argues that we frame our actions as 'serious' or as 'play.' Conversational participants can frame their talk as humorous by signaling 'This is play'" (2007:31). Shawn and Amber signal the humorous nature of their talk about *Extreme Makeover* with shared laughter, repetition, and increasing exaggeration of the hypothetical scenario. The success of this frame illustrates both that the speakers are employing shared norms of communication, since they are able to recognize each other's signals that this is not serious talk, and that they are engaged at least temporarily in conversational collaboration, rather than the strictly question-answer format often associated with interviews. According to Coates, "[c]ollaboration is an essential part of playful talk, since conversational participants have to recognise that a play frame has been invoked and then have to choose to maintain it" (32). She goes on to note that, "because conversational humour is a joint activity, involving all participants at talk, many commentators see its chief function as being the creation and maintenance of solidarity" (32). Thus, this interview is remarkable for its collaborative production, in the first and last sections.

Also noteworthy is the individual breakthrough into narrative performance that occurs in Shawn's long portion of talk in the middle of the interview. In any act of communication, performance can emerge to a greater or lesser extent: "[P]erformance is a variable quality, relatively more or less salient among the multiple functions served by a communicative act" (Bauman 1992:44). Bauman explains that "[t]he relative dominance of performance" as an aspect of communication "will depend on the degree to which the performer assumes responsibility to an audience for a display of communicative skill and effectiveness as against other communicative functions" (44). Similar to play frames, performances are marked by speakers and, in situations where participants share an understanding of communicative practices, recognized by audiences (45). In Amber's interview of Shawn, she recognizes that his breakthrough into an extended story ensures him the right to maintain the speaking floor, and she refrains from taking a turn at talk. During the performative narrative that dominates a half hour of his interview, Shawn describes the progression of events after his arrival at work, from the flooding of the prison to the inmates' evacuation onto a highway overpass. His skill as a narrator ensures him the opportunity and the audience to convey his significant message: during Katrina, laypeople did not have access to information, and those in authority who did have information failed to use it appropriately.

Shawn works skillfully at re-creating a scene in which information was scarce and withheld via a narrative in which information is plentiful and freely shared. At one point in Shawn's story, he is describing the events inside of the jail building on the level, or "tier," where he was working, and he begins to explain how outside law enforcement was brought into an already confusing and tense situation:

> [T]he SWAT team actually came in; they pulled me off the tier and they asked me who was giving the problems, you know, on each dorm. And I let them know because they wanted to come in on them, you know, and try to start some kind of control, establish some kind of control and discipline, you know to try to control the situation. 'Cause obviously this was happening in each jail, you know, and they finally made it to our jail. (Shawn 2008)

First, Shawn depicts the dramatic entry of the SWAT team, who "actually" came in and who "pulled him" from his post. Shawn's use of "actually" in this sentence suggests both actuality—they really did come in—and the connotative meaning of surprise, as in "believe it or not, this actually happened." This language implies Shawn did not expect their arrival and was unaware of their plan of action. The tables quickly turn, however, and it is not the young deputy who is without knowledge, but rather the newly arrived officials who are inquiring about the situation at hand, at which point Shawn is willing to "let them know" what he knows. Shawn then repeats three times what he understands as the SWAT team's mission, to "establish some kind of control." Control is linked to knowledge: the people who know what is going on are in control. Finally, Shawn explains that "obviously this was happening in each jail," regaining his own control of the narrative by demonstrating that he now has knowledge exceeding what he knew at the time and by sharing knowledge that goes beyond what his interviewer or potential extended audience might know.

As the story continues, actions take on added significance given Shawn's thematic foregrounding of information as a tool of control: "and [the SWAT team] was up there by me and they came in, they bust through the doors, you know, shooting the bean bag guns, everybody was on the floors and stuff, and it worked for a little while, you know ... They made them stay in the bed and they ain't want to move. Like I said, that worked for a little while" (Shawn 2008). Here, the SWAT team's actions are temporarily effective because they are shooting bean bag guns, which create the illusion that they are using deadly weapons on the inmates. In other interviews from the SKRH collection, witnesses describe seeing a gun being fired, then a person falling down. The witnesses' first interpretation is that the person has been shot and killed; it is only later that they realize the gun is firing hard bean bags, which strike with enough force to stun someone and knock them over, but not kill them. Here, the SWAT team is intentionally creating a situation where misinformation lends them momentary control: if the inmates think they are being fired at, they will not move.

While Shawn sympathetically portrays both deputies and inmates as being at an informational disadvantage, he does not extend the same explanation of behavior to officials such as the SWAT team and, later in his narrative, the sheriff and the attorney general. Unlike in the dominant discourse, where the almost entirely African American prison population was shown as threatening, in Shawn's narrative, the real threat was in the hands of authority figures with their mishandling of information. He describes the behavior of the prison's inmates in these terms:

[W]e have to run from this floor to that floor, to this dorm to that dorm, try—
'cause people done broke windows and actually trying to get out. You know, so
we have to wrestle with some of these people ... when they saw all of us, they
still—they was like, "Y'all gonna have to kill us because we not gonna just sit up
here and be treated the way we being treated." When in actuality they didn't know
what was really going on, you know. They ain't know what we was going through,
either. (Shawn 2008)

Shawn implies that had the inmates had knowledge of the reasons for the flooding, chaos, and lack of food and water, they would have acted differently. Their "threatening" behavior, made much of in national news reports, is explained, according to Shawn, by the fact that they did not understand everyone else was suffering as well. However, other actors in his story who have knowledge of suffering and do not act accordingly are portrayed in a less favorable light: "[W]e listening and—who we hear on the radio? Sheriff: 'Well, I didn't tell those deputies that came in to come to work. They volunteered to come to work.' You know. We volunteered? . . . If this was voluntary I damn sure wouldn't be here" (Shawn 2008). In this case, not only did the sheriff not use the information he had to protect his employees before and during the hurricane, but he then publicly offered misinformation about their experiences to make himself unaccountable, contributing to misrepresentation in the national discourse on Katrina.

Shawn's rhetorical strategies help his audience situate him as an actor in relationship to information. In their chapter in *Responsibility and Evidence in Oral Discourse*, Jane Hill and Ofelia Zepeda describe how narrators work at preserving a positive image of themselves by managing the dissemination of responsibility for problematic events. In Hill and Zepeda's example, the speaker "uses a variety of rhetorical devices to reduce the likelihood that she will be held 'personally responsible' for the 'trouble' she addresses . . . The effect of these devices is a representation of responsibility as 'distributed' in a complex social field, rather than concentrated in a single agent" (1993:197). The "complex social field" includes both the characters in the narrative, or the "story world," and the "interactional world," or the context in which the story is being told (197).[5] Employing similar tactics to Hill and Zepeda's speaker, Shawn distributes the responsibility for the troubling events that unfold in his story about the flooded prison. One of these tactics is the use of reported speech, as in Shawn's recollection of the sheriff's statement on the radio. This locates responsibility both in the story world, with the dishonest sheriff, and in the storytelling context; as Hill and Zepeda demonstrate, audiences are less likely to directly dispute "constructed dialogue,"[6] thereby enabling "complicity with the interlocutor" (197). Similar to Shawn, Hill and Zepeda's narrator "represents herself as being unable to influence directly the course of events . . . because she lacks the necessary knowledge at crucial junctures" (198). Shawn's narrative of Katrina creates a "story world" wherein other people are irresponsible in their manipulation of information, and an "interactional world" where he is a responsible narrator who openly shares information with his audience.

When Shawn *does* withhold information, it only furthers his presentation of himself as someone who does not engage in the dangerous information mismanagement that his story describes. At one point in his extended narrative, he allows his story to lead the listener to surprise:

> And we had a back-up call downstairs, and I remember running down the steps, and I just—I was coming off the second floor and I was coming down the steps and—*shwoom*—I slipped in the water. I say Lord, they got water coming up to the second floor. And I fell down the steps into the water, and [chuckles] it was funny—well it's funny now, but it wasn't funny then 'cause I'm like, man this water not stopping, you know. (Shawn 2008)

Here, Shawn creates suspense with his repetition in the first two lines, drawing out the action of running down the steps. He then provides a dramatic sound effect followed by the sudden, "I slipped in the water." This is surprising to the listener not only because of the buildup that precedes it, but because this is his first mention of the water being at that level inside the building. He has his listener encounter the flooding just as he did: unaware and at full speed. This kind of withholding information, however, is immediately tempered by humor as Shawn invites his listener to laugh with him at something that is "funny now" even though "it wasn't funny then." Shawn manages the distribution of information strategically, then, but the effects are presented as harmless, even humorous, as opposed to life threatening.

Bauman writes:

> ... [S]tories, like all literature used as equipment for living (Burke 1941), have a certain metaphorical as well as metonymic meaning ... as a kind of extended name or label for the recurrent social problem situations they portray ... And to extend the Burkean perspective still further, the stories also convey an attitude toward such situations and a strategy for dealing with them. (1986:77)

In his Katrina story, Shawn conveys that the lack of information available to laypeople was a problem and his impression that these people—himself included—acted accountably given the circumstances, contrary to their depiction in the national news and public imagination. Finally, this interview gives him space to express his belief that a more responsible management of information is an appropriate strategy for dealing with situations like the one he endured.

"It Worked Out": Patrice's Story

Listening to Shawn's narrative together with Patrice's reinforces that an interactional context with an empathetic listener and shared communicative norms enables Katrina survivors to situate themselves in a better light than that cast by popular public discourse.[7] Patrice gave two interviews about her experiences of Katrina. The first interview, conducted by Adele, was done in January 2006; it lasts about forty-two minutes. The second interview was ten months later, in November 2006; conducted by Sheryl, it is fifty-six minutes long. Patrice's second interview is different in that it is characterized by a slower pace and more explicit interviewer interest in Patrice's pre-Katrina life; the result is a narrative more reflective of Patrice's logic and responsibility in the face of the storm.

In the first interview, from January, Patrice's narration is confused and does not communicate a sense of control over her post-Katrina actions. The interviewer sets a quick pace with her first four questions, asking the following all within the first minute of talk: "How are you doing?" "Where did you live before Katrina?" "Where were you the day of the storm?" and "How long before the storm struck did you know about it?" (Patrice 2006a). Patrice gives equally quick answers, and then Adele follows with, "Okay. Can you tell me what happened the day the storm struck?" (Patrice 2006a). Her use of "okay" here suggests that she is ready to move on, perhaps to what she sees as the real reason for the interview, the events that occurred during the hurricane itself. The other questions appear as a brief formality to establish Patrice's whereabouts for what quickly emerges as the main event. Patrice, who has responded consistently with the tempo of the first few questions, hesitates with this new open-ended format. She replies, "Well, when the—when it—when the storm was coming, like that—I'm trying to think of the days. The storm was on that Monday?" (Patrice 2006a). Having jumped from the present moment ("How are you doing?") to her pre-Katrina life ("Where did you live before Katrina?") to the storm itself ("Where were you the day of the storm?") in less than a minute's time, Patrice is understandably disoriented. She exhibits this by searching for words, struggling with recollection of the exact day, and, finally, seeking confirmation—"the storm was on that Monday?" Rather than confirming Patrice's hesitant query, however, Adele disagrees and says the storm was on Tuesday. They go back and forth for a moment, until Patrice gains certainty and declares (correctly), "It was Monday" (Patrice 2006a). With this statement, she begins her first segment of extended narrative, describing her initial knowledge of the storm and her discovery that the city was flooding.

As the first interview proceeds, however, Patrice continues to question herself with frequent false starts and repairs. Her narrative jumps in both chronology and location, and reported speech threatens to take over the logical progression of her story. When she describes how her sister called to inform her of the storm's severity, Patrice starts to recount a conversation that she says happened that Monday: "And my sister, she called me. She was like, 'Girl, you'—No. I take that back. Like that part—the day before the storm, my sister called me, and she said, 'What you doing, you better get out'" (Patrice 2006a). Perhaps Adele's initial questioning of Patrice's memory has instilled doubt in the narrator's mind about her ability to accurately recount her experience. Patrice's rapid movement between different times and places also reflects the pattern set by the first few minutes of interviewing. She continues to describe the days around the storm as follows:

> The day after the storm, that's when the water started coming . . . Cause the storm was over when that—before that water, I mean—the water came. And so like I had my four kids, my nephew, and I had this little baby that I had accumulated in the storm . . . We had food and stuff. Like I said, my neighbor, they had a generator and we used that, and it lasted till like four o'clock that, that Wednesday morning . . . And I was like, "Oh, when the water go down tomorrow"—cause I knew my friend, she said she wasn't going away, and she—I say, "I got to go check on [Cathy]." And then I say, "My friend, [Nicole]," or whatever, so I said, "I got to go check on [Nicole]." But the water never went down. And the amazing part of it was—the same way the people was trying to separate the men and the women, and stuff. (Patrice 2006a)

In this brief segment of speech, Patrice moves back and forth between Tuesday, Wednesday, Monday, and an unspecified stretch before and after (from "I knew my friend . . . wasn't going away" to "the water never went down"). She also intersperses activity at her house, a neighbor's, and her friends' homes. Perhaps most out of place chronologically and geographically is her concluding comment, which alludes to a much later series of events when evacuees are struggling to get on buses at the highway overpass where she and her family will end up later that week. After she mentions it here, however, she goes back into explaining who was in her home with her, and she does not pick up this dangling narrative thread until about five minutes later in the interview.

Patrice also includes the words of others in such a way and to such an extent that the reported speech almost overwhelms her narration. When continuing to describe how she first heard that the city was in danger of flooding, Patrice recounts the following:

> So, one of my other friends, well she called me . . . she said . . . "you better get out of there." I said, "Girl, let me call you back. My sister just called me talking about twenty feet of water." So I said, "Twenty feet of water, twenty feet of water." I said, "They said they had a forty feet surge and twenty feet of water was coming

out of the, the river, or wherever it was coming from." So I said, "Twenty feet of water. That mean it got to be distributed among the whole city." So I said, "Well, it ain't going to be that bad. We probably got like two feet by the time it get to us." (Patrice 2006a)

In this excerpt, Patrice incorporates the words of her friend, her sister, and an unidentified "they," which most likely refers to newscasters.[8] She includes her own thought process as reported speech, which relegates her own knowledge at the time to one voice in a confusing sea of voices. With laughter at the end of this account, Patrice also distances her present self, as the narrator who now knows better, from the self who mistakenly believed that "twenty feet of water" referred to the total amount that would flood the city and that it would be "distributed" so that it would not exceed two feet in her neighborhood. However, this hint of distance between Patrice as a narrator in the interview situation and Patrice as the actor in her hurricane story is not sufficient to counter the confused portrayal of her actions, which resonates in some ways with the news media's reductive depiction of African American hurricane survivors as helpless victims. In her second interview, though, Patrice is able to contradict that dominant narrative by presenting her actions as logical in their consistency with her belief system, as well as responsible and compassionate in the care they demonstrate for her family and other survivors.

The interview that Patrice gives ten months after her first one is more coherent, includes more fluid sentences and a more straightforward chronology, and contains more moments of reflection on and evaluation of the experience being narrated. These changes may in part be due to the greater amount of time that has passed since the storm, as well as the different style of interaction that occurs with the second interviewer. Patrice's second interview, conducted by Sheryl, gets off to a much more gradual start than the first one. For the first four minutes of the interview, Sheryl asks questions that build on each other in eliciting a description of Patrice's life prior to Katrina. The series of questions is as follows: "Tell me a little bit about your life in New Orleans; where did you live?"; "And what did you guys do out there? What was your neighborhood like?"; "And did you—did you like living in this area?"; "Did—what kind of things did you guys do—activities, for fun?" (Patrice 2006b). This sequence is more chronologically and geographically consistent than the first interviewer's opening questions, and these questions follow an open-ended pattern (after the first one, which Patrice answers with three words) and demonstrate a bit of hesitation on the part of the interviewer. This line of questioning produces longer, more coherent answers from Patrice, and when the interviewer finally asks about the storm ("And, where—where—what were—what was going on when you first heard about the storm?"), Patrice responds with more than five minutes of uninterrupted talk (Patrice 2006b). Patrice also prefaces her first reaction to the news of the storm by describing both the prevailing beliefs about hurricanes in the city ("they call New Orleans 'The Big Easy,' and I think we kind of like thought that it was going to be what it always was, that the storm is coming and the storm never comes") as well as her own belief system ("I have faith in God and I know that, you know, our beginning and our endings are mandated by Him") (Patrice 2006b). In this way, Patrice builds up a logical narrative frame for her reluctance to evacuate, a decision that she reflects on more explicitly in this version of her narrative.

One factor in her initial decision to stay, which Patrice reiterates in both versions of her story, is her religious faith.[9] Early on in both interviews, Patrice shares the concerns she had at the time because her children do not share her trust in God. In the first interview, Patrice explains her doubt as follows:

> And I was getting a little paranoid or whatever, so I was like, "Lord"—you know, like, you know, cause I, I'm a Christian, and I'm like, "I hope I'm not being selfish, you know, making my kids stay here," or whatever, you know, "because maybe they don't—you know, they don't know You like I know You," so I was like, "Oh, my God." So he was like, "Don't worry about it. I got your back." So I was like, "Well, we going to, we going to stay," or whatever. (Patrice 2006b)

In this account, Patrice uses false starts, qualifiers, and hedging ("a little paranoid," "I, I'm a Christian," "maybe they don't—you know, they don't know You"). These qualities of her speech might suggest hesitation at the time of the events being narrated; she is reliving the worry that made her wonder whether she was right in acting on a faith not shared by her children. The later iteration of this story, however, reveals a different picture of her doubt.

In the second interview, Patrice describes the role of faith in her decision in the following words:

> I don't really like to push religion on people, and I don't force it on my kids, so some kind of way I feel, you know I feel kind of like bad because—because what I believe in I didn't want to—I felt like I had forced it on them, and I felt like I had kind of like jeopardized their situation because of what I believe in God, and so I was like, "Oh Lord, I made my children stay here, and I'm depending on you." And it was like, and I—and I, you know, you know, and God said, "If you don't hear my voice, just pay attention to my plan." So basically, that's what I had to do. I just had to pay attention to his plan and it worked out. It worked out. (Patrice 2006b)

In this case, Patrice's concern becomes less about the difference between her faith and that of her children, and more about the responsibility that making that decision for them places on her. She makes explicit here the fear that she had "jeopardized their situation because of what [she] believe[s]." Consistent with the overall tone of this second interview, Patrice offers reflection about the experiences she is recounting. Again, this may be influenced by the time that has elapsed, giving her distance to examine her motivations and build a logical narrative out of scattered memories. But it is also a result of the interview context, wherein Patrice's narrative is first grounded in a conversation that leads up to the troubling events of the hurricane and is then slowly elicited with open-ended questions.

In the second interview, Patrice emerges as a more competent narrator—and, consequently, a more competent actor in the story about her experience. In the first example above, she is being "paranoid" and possibly "selfish," making a decision marked by a great deal of ambiguity: "So I was like, 'Well, we going to, we going to stay,' or whatever." The qualifications surrounding her decision lend it uncertainty and convey doubt on Patrice's part about whether her choice was in her children's best interest. The more contemplative tone in the second account moves from doubt in her decision to a larger (and more removed) moral question about whether it is acceptable to "force" religion on other people, especially one's children. In this narrative, Patrice still reveals her doubt, but only in a passing moment; her fear for her children is quickly mitigated by her faith, and her decision is validated when she repeats—twice, for emphasis—"it worked out."

In both interviews, Patrice also recalls her horror at the treatment of elderly people who were waiting to be rescued on the highway overpass in Metairie, just outside city limits.[10] In the earlier telling, the narrative unfolds in this way:

You know, and then Metairie, where they dropped us off at, you know, it was just, it was horrible. The old people was on the ground. They were stepping on them. One lady I can remember her like she was my mama. She say, "You all keep stepping on me," until she didn't even open up her mouth no more. She just laid there. And the young folks, they just walked all over these old people because nobody was making arrangements for the old people to get on the bus before the younger people. Now, if you want to talk about fair is fair, with the women and the babies, I think the elderly people should have been a priority, and they was not a priority at all. I seen them … you know, dirty clothes and just shit—excuse me—on them and stuff. And nobody even cared. Nobody even stopped to say, you know, "Can I help you?" Or whatever. Nobody did. (Patrice 2006a)

In the later interview, this same scene emerges with its terribly memorable details, but cast in a slightly different light:

> I feel bad for the old people, like when they took us you know in the helicopter and then we went under—what street is that—Causeway, they were stepping on the old people, you know. It's like nobody cared. And I'm like, "Do y'all see y'all stepping on these people?" You know, they couldn't move. And it was like, one lady, they just stepped on her so much, she didn't even look up no more. I guess the lady was like, well it's just not going even do me a bit of good, because she didn't have no energy, she was old and she couldn't fight nobody; you know it was—it was no sense of urgency. (Patrice 2006b)

In both accounts, Patrice focuses on one elderly woman in particular, the one who persists in her memory like her own mother. In the first interview, Patrice recalls that the woman on the ground said, "You all keep stepping on me." In the later recollection, though, the older woman says nothing, and it is Patrice who remarks, "Do y'all see y'all stepping on these people?" In both versions, the scene ends with the utter hopelessness of the old woman giving up and lying on the ground while younger people literally walk over her. However, in Patrice's later narrative, the change in voice marks a change in accountability: Patrice herself emerges as one person who does care, who will say something to help the woman. Furthermore, at this point in the interview, Patrice transitions from her remark about "no sense of urgency" into a critique of government and media agencies. Thus, the problem shifts outwardly from the lack of compassionate response from those at the scene to a more general failure on the part of disaster response officials. In this way, much like Shawn in his tale about the prison flooding, Patrice is able to distribute responsibility to "a complex social field" in this second interview (Hill and Zepeda 1993).

"Like in a Movie": Additional Discursive Contexts

Shawn and Patrice, like other participants in SKRH, use rhetorical strategies to contend with pernicious, widespread public narratives. However, SKRH narrators also occasionally invoke larger discourses that do not necessarily cast them in a negative light. At one point in his interview, Shawn struggles to find the right words to describe the blacked-out, flooded city where he spent the night on a highway overpass:

[A]ll through the night you just hear gunfires. And I don't know if you've ever been outside when it's just pitch black, but being on the interstate, and they don't have no light in your city—that's like a weird feeling. It's like—like, like in a movie or something, you know. And I'm just fortunate that I had a weapon because I felt just a little bit more comfortable than the next man who didn't have one to protect they self, you know. (Shawn 2008)

Searching for a familiar basis for comparison, an image that might render this frightening world legible, Shawn concludes that his situation was "like in a movie." Other survivors echo this general reference to movies, without specifying a particular film or even genre.

Shawn's attempt to interpret a new and strange experience by referring to popular culture is not unusual; rhetorician Barry Brummett theorizes that popular culture provides people with "reservoirs of ways to manipulate signs, of the logics one might use to make meaning" (1991:77). Brummett describes an indistinct rhetorical backdrop, what he calls "conditional rhetoric," as "a ghost haunting the houses of 'real' texts, faintly seen assumptions and conditions hovering just beyond the clear and concrete signs and utterances of speeches and everyday life" (46). He proposes that "shadow texts," the manifestations of conditional rhetoric, are implied by other, obvious communicative texts. Although Brummett suggests that these "shadow texts" only exist via their influence on more discrete (clearly bounded) texts, folklorist Jay Mechling draws on the model to explain the intertextual referencing of one discrete text by another: "'Shadow texts' . . . [are] the familiar texts we bring to our experiences with new texts. Shadow texts help determine—perhaps they overdetermine—our understandings of the newly encountered text. The intertextual conversation sometimes happens against our will" (2004:51).[11] Mechling notes that popular culture can be a source of shadow texts, helping to explain why Shawn might think of "a movie" when faced with the inexplicable scenario he encountered after Katrina.

In terms familiar to folklorists accustomed to considering performers' repertoires, a narrator's accumulation of popular culture images and logics can be thought of as a "storehouse of imaginative materials available to each person [that] provides a sort of repertoire. . . . The reservoir of acquired models exerts a strong influence both upon perception and upon response to unfamiliar models" (Novak qtd. in Brummett 1991:102). This conceptualization also helps to extend Brummett's and Mechling's analyses, beyond the act of interpretation to the act of performance. Popular culture texts not only help Shawn and others make meaning of Katrina's events, they aid in communicating that meaning to others. Shawn's imprecise allusion to a movie scene works effectively to justify his emotions and actions in the narrative. He creates a more familiar world for his listener, invoking a dramatic sensation of fear, so when he goes on to note that he needed a weapon to feel comfortable, it is a reasonable claim in that context. Drawing on familiar popular culture representations of dangerous settings, however vaguely, works to Shawn's narrative advantage.

In addition to lending familiar imagery and emotion to his account, though, Shawn's movie reference suggests alienation from his own experience. Another refrain echoed in SKRH interviews is that what survivors witnessed "didn't seem real"; rhetorically, this assessment, together with the movie comparison, reinforces that these experiences are ones that survivors had only previously conceived of in fictional terms, if at all. This might substantiate what they witnessed, an important claim for credibility in the face of incredulous audiences: something along the lines of, "I know it's hard to believe. I couldn't believe it myself." Statements like this also indicate that in some ways, with respect to the horrible events they saw, they were spectators, rather than participants. Just as with other rhetorical strategies discussed above, this perspective helps to deflect responsibility for the atrocities that transpired. This is not to say that Shawn or any other narrators are evading blame that *should* be placed on them, but rather that they are wary of being seen as at fault for the suffering they describe. In many ways, then, these interview narratives provide speakers with the opportunity to position themselves—and sometimes they position themselves as watching, astonished, just like the rest of us.

Conclusion

The SKRH interviews provide a unique communicative context: the people in conversation are, in many geographic and social senses of the word, from the same community of New Orleans and are now part of a new community of evacuees in Houston. They are also, as the design of the project suggests, likely to empathize with each other as survivors of the same disaster. As evidenced in Shawn's interview and Patrice's second interview, these commonalities have the potential to enable remarkable communicative events, marked by collaboration, and by competence in both narration and, retrospectively, in action. Shawn is able to manage the information that was withheld from him during the storm and present himself as someone who acted responsibly with the knowledge he had. In her second interview, Patrice reflects on her decisions to explain them in the context of her belief systems, and she presents herself as compassionate. Where communicative norms are not shared, as in Patrice's first recording, the narratives reflect incomprehensibility and self-doubt. Furthermore, with the creation of rapport in the interview setting, narrators enact the distribution of responsibility for troubling events, and what Hill and Zepeda call the "complicity with the interlocutor" (1993:197) strengthens the bonds between interview participants. In these representative interviews, empathetic collaboration and shared communicative norms enable the emergence of a narrative in which speakers position themselves favorably in relation to the events they describe, whether that puts them in the center of the action or places them at a remove, like a skeptical spectator. In a documentation project where the object is to allow individuals to tell their own stories, on their own terms, these stories are positive results. They allow speakers to contradict their negative portrayals in public discourse with their own versions of themselves: not criminals, not helpless victims, but responsible employees, good parents, and caring neighbors.

Carl Lindahl, along with others, has publicized the success of SKRH and advocated for applying its lessons and methods in other contexts of disaster response. The stories of nine SKRH interviewees are included in *Second Line Rescue: Improvised Responses to Katrina and Rita* (Ancelet, Gaudet, and Lindahl 2013), with context and reflection provided by the interviewers. Honoring the wishes of many project contributors, the volume presents these accounts as evidence against the criminalizing discourse of Katrina's media coverage—evidence that illustrates more broadly how disaster is likely to bring out "uncommon grace and goodness" (Lindahl 2013:250; see also Solnit 2009) in people rather than drive them to violence and chaos.

Elsewhere, Lindahl makes a more explicit case for widely applying the methods of SKRH (2012b). In the case of Katrina, legends perpetuated by authority figures and circulated by news outlets depicted survivors as a threat to potential rescuers. On the other hand, legends shared among survivors suggested that authorities had intentionally blown up levees protecting New Orleans's poorest neighborhoods to divert flooding from richer residents and business and tourism districts. Despite the historical precedent for intentional flooding of Louisiana's impoverished communities (documented in 1927 and suspected in 1965), and despite the lack of evidence that survivors engaged in behavior such as shooting at helicopters, "media truth remained psychologically true long after its assertions had been discredited [while] the psychological truths of the victims were dismissed out of hand" (Lindahl 2012b:149).[12] This narrative inequality translates directly to ineffective disaster response: survivors are mischaracterized as a threat, causing officials to delay their rescue efforts, blaming those most in need of aid for its deferral. Then those same survivors' legitimate concerns about threats to their well-being are, to put it mildly, disbelieved—viewed as further proof of their unworthiness. To interrupt this cycle, "[t]he demonstrably effective tools fashioned by folklorists and perfected by survivors in the SKRH project offer the single best opportunity to refute and counteract the effects of negative legendry, to give survivors the opportunity to own their own stories" (Lindahl 2012b:172–73). This model of survivor-led documentation and recovery is already proving to be effective in other disaster-response efforts around the world.[13] But the goals and methods of this project are transferrable in other ways as well: the tactics successfully employed by SKRH participants should serve as a model in any context where personal narratives about disaster are collaboratively produced for a public audience. In more widely circulated publications where the context of narrative production is concealed, such as those in the following chapters, collaboration gives way to exploitation and reinforcement of negative, stereotypical representations of Katrina survivors.

CHAPTER TWO

From "Angel of Mercy" to "Fallen Folk Hero": Zeitoun's Story Travels

Genres of public narrative beyond news media shape opinions about, responses to, and memories of disaster. Two books published to popular acclaim, Dave Eggers's *Zeitoun* and Josh Neufeld's *A.D.: New Orleans after the Deluge*, have entered powerfully into public dialogue about the hurricane.[1] *Zeitoun* is a work of literary nonfiction focused on the dramatic story of one Katrina survivor, and *A.D.* (the subject of the following chapter) is a nonfiction graphic novel portraying the hurricane-related experiences of seven New Orleanians. Both books draw on the personal narratives of real survivors in attempts to communicate to a public audience about this catastrophic event. Both succeed in artistic terms, producing well-received, high-quality work in many regards. Ultimately, though, as these personal narratives about communal trauma go public, individuals morph into stereotypes, and audiences disregard the complexities of the actual people involved in favor of familiar stories they already know. Thus, Denise in *A.D.* is interpreted as a stereotypical African American woman raging ineptly and inappropriately at her circumstances. And Abdulrahman Zeitoun is first celebrated as an American hero after the publication of Eggers's book, then later vilified as a violent Muslim when charges of domestic violence emerge.

Abdulrahman Zeitoun (who goes primarily by his last name) is a Syrian American contractor who spent most of his adult life in New Orleans with his wife and children. Zeitoun's choice to stay in New Orleans during Hurricane Katrina resulted in a nightmare scenario: his home and neighborhood flooded, he witnessed the abandonment of his neighbors while attempting to aid in their rescue, and ultimately, he was wrongfully imprisoned for three and a half weeks. Zeitoun's story circulates well: audiences are intrigued, outraged, and sympathetic, especially when reading of his ordeal in the widely popular *Zeitoun*, written by Dave Eggers and published in 2009. Before *Zeitoun*, there were other versions of this story. The human rights organization Voice of Witness, of which Eggers is cofounder, orchestrated interviews with Katrina survivors for their collection *Voices from the Storm*. According to their records, Zeitoun was interviewed by Lola Vollen and Billy Sothern. *Voices of the Storm* (coedited by Vollen) was published in 2006 and includes excerpts of the interview with Zeitoun. Billy Sothern, an anti–death penalty lawyer, published *Down in New Orleans* in 2007, including a chapter detailing Zeitoun's experiences and quoting from the same interview. Before those three books hit the shelves, a first-person blog chronicling Zeitoun's experiences appeared on the NOLA.com website. The blog entry was published online in November 2005, only two months after Zeitoun's release from the Hunt Correctional Center. Clearly this story appeals to people—authors, activists, audiences. But what happens to Zeitoun's story as it travels through these various venues of publication? It becomes what its genres demand and what its audiences expect to hear: the honest account of a hardworking immigrant, the unreliable voice of an emotional eyewitness, the tale of a foreigner who temporarily transforms into an all-American hero, and finally, the deceptive disguise of a violent Muslim man oppressing his wife.

One central element of Zeitoun's Katrina story is his arrest: he was snatched without explanation from his own property, informally accused of terrorism then formally accused of looting, held for three and a half weeks in multiple jail facilities, strip searched, robbed, interrogated, and denied basic rights including a phone call to his family, who meanwhile presumed him dead. He was eventually released on bail and continues to deal with the legal and personal repercussions of his incarceration—a mistake forged in the fires of panic, Islamophobia, and crippled bureaucracy. In all four narrative accounts, Zeitoun's first encounter with the officials who arrest him is crucial and compelling.

However, an earlier moment in the story is equally important in considering how Zeitoun is presented or how he presents himself.[2] Each text—blog, interviews, and book—includes a visually striking recollection where Zeitoun enters a house to rescue an elderly woman who is literally hanging on for her life, holding herself up by the furniture in her flooded home, surrounded by her billowing dress. This moment lends itself to retelling because its imagery is vivid and memorable. As Ulf Palmenfelt describes in his study of World War II narratives, one of the most often-repeated stories is one where a child uses his family's cherished ration book to purchase milk and then drops the jar of milk on the way back home. The story centers on the heart-wrenching image of the white milk spreading out over a cobblestone street (Palmenfelt 2011). In stories like these, the repeated visual element takes on the qualities of an icon—instantly recognizable, both symbolic and indexical in its representation of suffering. Whereas the spilled milk appears in a variety of stories told by different narrators, the floating woman appears in multiple renditions of the same story. Like the milk, though, the woman is almost unchanged across narrative versions.

The encounter with the elderly woman is also a crucial depiction of Zeitoun as the hero of this story. As Zeitoun paddles around flooded streets in his canoe, he and his friend hear the woman call out for help. Zeitoun goes to great lengths to rescue this woman, swimming up to her home, kicking down the swollen door, going to find more help because the woman is heavy and nearly immobile, and finally maneuvering her into a waiting boat. Given her age, gender, and frailty, she fits the quintessential description of a helpless victim, and Zeitoun's rescue efforts in this scenario serve as a dramatic counterpoint to his ensuing wrongful arrest and imprisonment. Seeing him as a hero on a mission enables the audience to fully sympathize with the obstacles he later faces. In each narrative version, Zeitoun reflects on the sense of purpose he feels after saving this woman, which lends varying degrees of heroic motive to his actions.

The Blog: "I Found This Old Lady"

Under the title "Rescue Efforts Lead to Arrest Nightmare for N.O. Businessman," Zeitoun's story appeared on a blog on NOLA.com on November 24, 2005. NOLA.com is the website associated with New Orleans's major newspaper, the *Times-Picayune*. Since the *Times-Picayune* reduced its print distribution to three days a week in 2012, NOLA.com has become a source for headline news; however, at the time of Zeitoun's blog, the site's contents were often more geared toward tourism and entertainment. Many of the blogs associated with the *Times-Picayune* and NOLA.com transformed into emergency communication or other community forums in the wake of the storm, with much of their content being provided by readers. The website was almost entirely focused on post-Katrina developments, and the blog in particular was dedicated to personal accounts of survival and recovery.

Zeitoun's entry is extensive, about twelve pages in length, and its first half is segmented into discrete days in the style of a journal. Zeitoun begins his blog by explaining that he is a local businessman, assuring readers that he has "a very good reputation throughout the city of New Orleans" and that he is "listed with the Better Business Bureau" (2005). Zeitoun has heightened cause to make these claims for his credibility; as William Labov suggests, Zeitoun's story defies believability because of the events that transpire within it, ironically the very events that make it a story worth sharing (1982). He has also been through an ordeal in which his reputation was disregarded, so he is reaffirming that measure of his identity. To invoke authority, he refers to official organizations and emphasizes hard work as his defining characteristic: "I started my life from scratch, and worked my way up to where I am now" (Zeitoun 2005). This claim also places him in a narrative framework recognizable to his (primarily local and American) audience, that of the hardworking immigrant whose bootstrap mentality has paid off in a successful business. This relatively positive stereotype may be intentionally conjured to counteract an alternative stereotype that plagued Zeitoun's post-Katrina nightmare, wherein he was suspected of terrorism because he is a Muslim man of Middle Eastern descent.

The scene describing the elderly woman's rescue emerges during the portion of Zeitoun's NOLA.com blog entry that recounts Wednesday, August 31. During Zeitoun's first trip in his canoe since the levee failure on the previous day, he sets out with the intention of checking on his rental properties and with the thought he may be able to "even help people if they needed help" (Zeitoun 2005). At the point where he and his friend encounter the woman, he writes the following: "[W]e heard this muffled scream coming from somewhere. We couldn't find where it was coming from. I think the only reason we heard it was because the streets were so quiet. We yelled out to it. Asking 'Where are you?' The muffled voice was found coming from a house on Nashville Ave" (2005).

Following their realization of where the cries for help were coming from, Zeitoun describes his rescue efforts as follows: "I hopped out the canoe and swam to the door. I tried to open it, but it was stuck. The lady inside kept yelling 'Please help me! Please help me!' I kicked her door and finally got it open. I found this old lady in a one-story house, floating on her back, holding on to a piece of furniture calling for help. I told her I came to help her" (2005). This version of the discovery is essentially matter-of-fact; it moves bluntly from problem to solution with little added emotional content. This is not to say the narrative is not a moving one, but rather to point out its simplicity and focus on action.

Finally, Zeitoun narrates his levelheaded response to the crisis in which he finds the woman:

She said she can't swim. I grabbed hold of her and tried to pull her out of the house. She was a heavyset woman, so it was very hard. When I got her out of her house, I told her to hang on to her porch railing. She said "Please don't leave me, please don't leave me." I told her, "I can't put you in the canoe, it might flip." I promised her that we would be back with help. She yelled "I can't hold on very long. Please hurry, please hurry!" I got back in my canoe and we continued up Nashville [Avenue] to look for help. As much as I was happy to have this little canoe, was as much as I hated that it was so small. (2005)

In this manner, Zeitoun sums up his first attempt to rescue the woman, his realization that he and his friend could not do it alone, and his decision to seek out more help. After this, he goes on to recount how they finally found a larger boat with helpful civilians aboard—though they were passed up by several official first responders—and together the men managed to get the woman onto the larger boat and take her to safety. Quoted speech in this version portrays Zeitoun as rather straightforward and forceful, and the woman appears nearly hysterical; he describes her as "yelling" and in his quoted language she repeats everything twice. Finally, what Labov and Waletzky (1967) call the evaluation—the point of the story according to its narrator—can be found in Zeitoun's poignant remark that "as much as I was happy to have this little canoe, was as much as I hated that it was so small." In other words, he feels good about being able to help but simultaneously unable to do enough.

The Interviews: "I See One Old Lady, Remind Me like My Grandma"

Zeitoun's narrative was later published in Billy Sothern's *Down in New Orleans: Reflections from a Drowned City* (2007). Sothern combines auto-biographical reflections with journalistic presentation of survivors' experiences and an explicit social critique—especially of Louisiana's prison system, of which Sothern is an outspoken opponent. A short chapter in the middle of the text conveys Zeitoun's experiences and quotes substantially from an interview with him. It is preceded by a segment on another man, Dan Bright, who Sothern's legal office successfully exonerated after he had been wrongfully sentenced to death.[3] In this context, Zeitoun's story is presented as one in a series of cases where an innocent man stands wrongfully accused. Just as Zeitoun drew on his professional accreditations to lend credibility to his blog, Sothern invokes his success as an attorney to bolster his presentation of Zeitoun as an innocent man. Sothern writes that "Hurricane Katrina spurred on the biggest prison crisis since Attica. Unlike Attica . . . the crisis in New Orleans has failed to create a meaningful conversation about the treatment of American prisoners" (2007:73). Sothern aims, in including stories like Bright's and Zeitoun's, to facilitate such a conversation.

Perhaps to attach a sympathetic face to his cause of prison reform, Sothern presents Zeitoun in a romanticized light, selecting quotations from his interview that paint the man as a sort of naïve poet. For instance, Sothern begins and ends this chapter by quoting Zeitoun's use of proverbs. Américo Paredes writes that the "proverb presents conventional wisdom in a neat package" (1964:219) and that a proverb is a "one-line folk poem" (219). Sothern opens by describing Zeitoun as having "values . . . grounded in an old saying from his native Syria, 'small stones support mountains,' which led him to stay in New Orleans during Katrina. He believed that he could help" (2007:87). He closes the chapter by describing Zeitoun's continued affection for his adopted land and his feeling that his experiences do not represent America: "'Each country, each house, has nice people there, and has dirty people there,' he told me, offering another Syrian proverb: 'Back home we say, "Each home has a toilet"'" (101). By prefacing the Zeitoun chapter with the chapter on Dan Bright, and by framing Zeitoun's narrative with proverbs, Sothern sets up an opposition between Zeitoun's knowledge and language (conventional, poetic) and his own (legal, official). Although Sothern does not explicitly assign value to one form of knowledge and language, there is an implicit hierarchy in the chapter. Early on, Sothern quotes Zeitoun as saying he left Syria because there was "'too much politics, confusion.'" This remark is immediately followed with a parenthetical explanation from Sothern: "(This 'confusion' was Syria's 1973 'October War' with Israel over the Golan Heights)" (87). In such moments, Sothern positions himself as the expert who will elucidate the unsophisticated commentary of the innocent—in all senses of the word—Zeitoun.

The interview with Sothern is the basis both for Sothern's chapter on Zeitoun and for the segments on Zeitoun in the collection *Voices from the Storm* (Vollen and Ying 2006). *Voices from the Storm* is one in a series of books edited by Dave Eggers, Lola Vollen and Chris Ying, and published by Voice of Witness and McSweeney's Books. The aim of the series is as follows: "Using oral history as a foundation, the series illustrates human rights crises through the stories of the men and women who experience them," which serves the dual purposes of "allow[ing] those most affected by contemporary social injustice to speak for themselves" and simultaneously educating readers who are "interested in a reality-based understanding of ongoing injustices."[4] The series editors are dedicated to the premise that circulating narratives of human rights abuses will bring attention to and presumably ameliorate those abuses. Identifying the books as addressing "human rights crises" already frames the events and narrators in certain ways, creating expectations associated with popular discourses of human rights. A reader of such a text will most likely expect to be moved and outraged by the stories, although perhaps not to identify with the narrators. The stories might carefully balance familiarity with exoticism in order to engender empathy without creating too much discomfort.[5] Before even encountering "those most affected" who are "speaking for themselves," readers are being instructed about how to listen.

Voices from the Storm gathers interviews with thirteen New Orleanians who survived the hurricane. The interviewees, five women and eight men, are from a wide range of ethnic backgrounds and professions; in terms of socioeconomic background, they tend toward working class. The interview excerpts are arranged chronologically, first offering snippets from each narrator's life prior to Katrina, then interweaving accounts from each narrator day by day from August 27 to September 4, then continuing with excerpts describing the week after the hurricane (September 5 to 11) and more broadly "weeks after," and closing with segments of interviews where narrators are "looking back" on their experiences. This fragmentation of interviews illustrates the book's emphasis on the storm's timeline and on an overarching, imposed narrative, rather than the wholeness and integrity of the individual stories shared by survivors. After the interview-based portion, the book concludes with a brief note about methodology and an extensive section of appendices.[6]

Between each chronologically arranged section there are editorial inserts, including sketched images of each narrator accompanied by minibios, maps, and a bulleted list of what the editors viewed as key context for each section of interviews. For instance, the introductory page for Monday, August 29, explains, "At 8:14 a.m., the National Weather Service warns of a breach in the Industrial Canal" (Vollen and Ying 2006:73). These notes, in addition to the several appendices, presumably serve as guideposts for the reader, who may encounter conflicting memories from narrators, or who may doubt the veracity of these accounts without the authoritative framework that bolsters them. As with Zeitoun's credentials from the Better Business Bureau, citing sources such as the National Weather Service validates stories of events that seem incredible. However, this framing erodes the narrators' authority rather than adding to it. Whereas Zeitoun makes himself more credible by referring to his good reputation, these inserts imply a lessened credibility of interviewees by insisting on the need to substantiate their accounts with facts and figures. The inclusion of these materials suggests that, from the editors' perspective, the narrators are incapable of establishing credibility on their own. Similar to Sothern's hierarchical presentation of his expertise over Zeitoun's folk wisdom, the authority asserted by this volume's framing devices undermines the authority of the narratives themselves.

The editorial inserts are problematic for other reasons. The September 4 page offers this quip: "New Orleans police kill at least five New Orleans residents on the Danziger Bridge *after those residents opened fire* on government contractors hired to repair the 17th Street Canal" (Vollen and Ying 2006:171, emphasis added).[7] Subsequent investigations and trial proceedings related to these incidents have revealed that the residents did not "open fire"; on the contrary, police shot six unarmed civilians, killing a man with mental disabilities and a teenager (McCarthy 2012). The "facts" framing the interviews are equally as subject to reconsideration and revision as a personal account might be, and the use of such framing devices creates a false sense of superiority when it comes to outsider, official knowledge as opposed to insider, informally recounted experience.

Framed in these ways, and presumably due as well to the interactional context of the interview, Zeitoun's narrative takes on a more passive and emotional tone in the interview quoted in *Down in New Orleans* and *Voices from the Storm*. When Zeitoun describes his rescue of the neighborhood woman from inside her home, he begins as follows: "We hear this quiet noise and we stop to hear, to see where the noise come from, and we start following the voice and we got to very small house, few houses before Claiborne, one-story house, and have like green awning, I remember" (Vollen and Ying 2006:120). In this version of their discovery of the woman, the woman signals her presence with a "quiet noise" as opposed to the "muffled scream" of the blog entry. Zeitoun continues, "To go closer, I have to jump from my canoe, jump to the water, and I open a screen door, go to the porch and I get to the house. Inside, I see one old lady, remind me like my grandma. Her dress full like a big balloon, floating in the water, and she's on her back holding to her furniture" (Vollen and Ying 2006:120). Zeitoun's narrative is both more elaborated and more subdued in this context. In contrast to the short, violent phrases of his blog (he kicks the door, she yells repeatedly), in this version Zeitoun enters the house with ease, and the woman barely makes a sound. In fact, he does not quote the woman at all in this section of the story. Whereas reported speech disappears from this version, emotionally laden content that was absent from the blog makes an appearance here. The metaphorical language Zeitoun uses to describe her helplessness—her dress floating around her "like a balloon"—juxtaposes the fragility and innocence of that childhood toy with the desperation of the woman hanging on for her life. It also evokes a sense of the bizarre, in that a balloon is a strange and unexpected object in a story of a flood; this has the effect of conveying the inexplicable nature of some things encountered by survivors. Even more explicitly in terms of emotional impact, Zeitoun tells his audience that this woman "remind me like my grandma." This statement not only confirms the woman's age and perhaps her weakness, but also the sense of obligation Zeitoun felt to help her.

Zeitoun wraps up this vignette as follows: "I drag her by her shoulder, and brought her outside through the door. No way to put her in the canoe. To save her would be to drown her if I tried put her in the canoe, because it would flip no question. And I take her to the porch to try to go get some help" (Vollen and Ying 2006:120). Whereas in the first account he used the small size of his canoe to represent both his feeling of pride in helping and his limited capacity to do so, here he expresses his frustration by remarking that "to save her would be to drown her." In this starkly poetic version of his narrative evaluation, Zeitoun places more emphasis on his inability to do enough.

The Book: "Like a Great Floating Flower"

Dave Eggers's *Zeitoun* is a work of literary nonfiction: instead of first-person blog or minimally edited interview, readers encounter a third-person narrative, a tale artfully crafted by a well-known writer that, according to its author, sticks to the true story of Zeitoun's experiences. *Zeitoun* begins with Abdulrahman's childhood in Syria and includes his world travels as a member of the Merchant Marine, his marriage to Kathy, and the growth of their family and their contracting business in New Orleans. The narrative centers on Zeitoun's decision to stay in New Orleans during Katrina, the actions he took to protect his properties and neighbors, and his wrongful arrest and imprisonment. This story gives far more background and depth than the other three versions, with the storm incorporated into the context of a life story. This version echoes the others, though, in its claims to truthfulness and its narrative representation of the rescue scene. The paratext[8] of *Zeitoun* is saturated with affirmations of credibility and fidelity. Whereas *Voices from the Storm* undermines narrators' credibility by indicating a necessity for external evidence, Eggers makes this same move but then insists that the narrative is related "through [Zeitoun's] eyes" (2009b:345). Claims such as this create the illusion of the interviewee having authority, but in fact Eggers has created a credible character of Zeitoun, portrayed in this literary work. Zeitoun transforms from narrator, to narrator *in absentia*, and Eggers's efforts to redeem his disappearance result in a characterization that becomes a character type. Zeitoun becomes the silent, long-suffering immigrant whose heroic actions are righteous in the face of his treatment by xenophobic Americans.

Life narratives, especially those about lives that are foreign to Western audiences, are often accompanied by "endorsements and authorizations in the form of introductions, prefaces, appendixes, and blurbs that guide the reception of the text," and as "public intellectuals confer authority on the narrator;

they both encourage and instruct the reader to read the text properly" (Whitlock 2007:20). Gillian Whitlock notes this pattern in autobiographical texts from or about Muslim cultures circulating in the Western literary marketplace. Though *Zeitoun* is an American-written biographical account of a Muslim American, it is still "highly valued for its exotic appeal and educational value, for the status it confers on the consumer as an enlightened, sympathetic, and politically correct individual, and for that comforting narcissistic recognition that denies difference across cultures" (Whitlock 2007:15). The authoritative framing of Zeitoun's story in Eggers's book confers this status, making Western readers feel a false sense of connection to a different culture and fostering indignation that allows readers to feel they have taken the side of the oppressed, without having to act on their behalf or recognize complicity in their oppression.

Zeitoun's characterization as a particular type moves beyond the story's paratextual framing to the narrative itself. Describing Zeitoun's rescue of his elderly neighbor, Eggers begins in this way: "As they were paddling . . . they heard a faint female voice. It was a kind of moan, weak and tremulous. . . . It was coming from a one-story house on Nashville. They coasted toward the front door and heard the voice again: 'Help me'" (2009b:109). The woman's voice has transformed from the blog's "muffled scream," to the interview's "quiet noise," to a "weak and tremulous" moan. Not only has the sound become increasingly meek and pleading, but it has also acquired a gender: before, it was a scream from an unidentified source; now, it is a "faint female voice." The dramatic necessity of Zeitoun's heroism is dependent on the dire circumstances of his quest—in Eggers's rendering of this tale, readers can instantly read this as a damsel in distress. The fact that she is an elderly woman might add to the appeal of this story for readers; Zeitoun poses no threat to popular conceptions of Western masculinity as he might if he were rescuing a young (white) maiden from the flood.

Zeitoun enters the house and sees the woman for the first time:

> Zeitoun dropped his paddle and jumped into the water. He held his breath and swam to the porch. . . . "Hello?" the voice said, now hopeful. He tried the front door. It was stuck. Zeitoun kicked the door. It wouldn't move. He kicked again. No movement. With the water now to his chest, he ran his body against the door. He did it again. And again. Finally it gave. (Eggers 2009b:109)

Zeitoun's forceful attempts to get into the house are reminiscent of those in his blog entry, rather than the toned-down actions in his interview account. The woman's reported speech has also reentered the account, but just barely, with her pleading "Hello?" In this version, however, Zeitoun's continued bursts of activity ("He kicked again") are interspersed with the inactivity of the door itself ("No movement"). While the language echoes Zeitoun's previous action-oriented statements, the narration also incorporates a new element of dramatic suspense. The scene continues: "Inside he found a woman hovering above him. She was in her seventies, a large woman, over two hundred pounds. Her patterned dress was spread out on the surface of the water like a great floating flower. Her legs dangled below. She was holding on to a bookshelf. 'Help me,' she said" (Eggers 2009b:110). The memorable image of the dress echoes the interview version of the story, but whereas Zeitoun described it as a balloon, Eggers uses the metaphor of "a great floating flower." This continues to capture the vulnerability of the woman evoked by the balloon comparison, but it loses its bizarre quality: a flower is not surprising at all—what more clichéd image is there to describe a woman awaiting a man's arrival? The woman being rescued and her rescuer both become generalized, in part because of the recognizable narrative tropes and metaphorical language, but also because Eggers leaves out the most personal emotional appeal that Zeitoun included in his earlier story: here, there is no reference to the woman reminding him of his grandmother.

Zeitoun's narrative evaluation also does not emerge as it does in the other contexts. At the comparable point in the story, where Zeitoun and his friend decide they need more help and a bigger boat to get the woman to safety, what previously served as evaluation serves here as a conflict to be resolved. Eggers writes, "No one knew what to do next. It would be very difficult to fit a woman of her size into the canoe.... The canoe would certainly capsize.... They had no choice but to leave her and find help.... She was unhappy to be left alone again, but there was no choice" (2009b:110). The narration goes on to describe their search for help, their success in getting the woman to safety, and before the story cuts over to Baton Rouge to describe Kathy Zeitoun's simultaneous experiences, the reader leaves Abdulrahman "alone in the canoe . . . soaked and exhausted" (114). Zeitoun's quandary is perhaps implied in the statement "there was no choice," but this evaluative statement obscures the conflicting emotions Zeitoun endured. Nowhere does this mininarrative grasp with the same concision the combination of utility and despair that Zeitoun expresses in previous narratives: "as much as I was happy to have this little canoe, was as much as I hated that it was so small," and "to save her would be to drown her."

In all four of these texts, the strategies used to convey credibility, emotional impact, and purpose evolve based on genre conventions and audience expectations. In the blog, Zeitoun appeals to external validations of his credibility and draws on popular conceptions of immigrants in America. He characterizes his rescue efforts matter-of-factly, portrays the woman he rescues as agitated and even somewhat difficult, and expresses ambiguity about his ability to help those in need. In *Down in New Orleans* and *Voices from the Storm*, Zeitoun's story is framed in ways that diminish the value of the interview—by deferring to discourses of legal expertise and "fact-checking"—treating it as secondary evidence to a story being told with more authority by others. In this context, the emphasis is on Zeitoun's personal relationship to the woman he rescued, and both her assertiveness and his are downplayed. Zeitoun introduces new metaphorical language with more explicit emotional content, and he emphasizes his feelings of futility during this experience. In *Zeitoun*, Eggers has the luxury of an established reputation, so he is free to take more liberties with the management of credibility. Rather than having to focus on external validation and a narrative evaluation that conveys this story's purpose, Eggers's challenge is to fit this story into a framework that readers will recognize. Thus, where Zeitoun is concerned with expressing authority, urgency, and finally ambiguity; and where human rights activists are concerned with presenting a sympathetic case that advances their cause; Eggers is concerned with creating a heroic character type, a suspenseful buildup, and, finally, a clear resolution.

"He Was Needed": Zeitoun's Reception

Shortly after *Zeitoun*'s publication, NPR aired an episode of *All Things Considered* titled "War on Terror, Katrina Intersect in *Zeitoun*." The episode uses the rescue scene described above to illustrate the dramatic appeal of the book. The show transitions from Eggers's audio clips to Zeitoun's, with the two voices edited into a continuous narrative by the show's host. The effect is a hybrid of the two storytelling styles, with Zeitoun's urgency and ambivalence and Eggers's clear sense of purpose. Eggers begins, "[H]e hears a faint voice, coming from a home, and . . . he was with a friend at that point, and they paddled up to the house and . . ." (Eggers 2009a). The recording cuts to Zeitoun's voice, distinguishable with its accented English: "[A]nd we start slowly follow the noise." The host interjects, "Zeitoun picks up the story from here." Zeitoun continues:

> I jump to the water, swim to her house, and got the door. I try force the door to open; I kick it to open. As soon I open I see the lady—she have one story house. And middle her living room, she have furniture all over covered with water. She holding to her dining room table and like she's—the water up to her shoulders. And her dress floating 'round her like—like flower or like umbrella, however you

going to say it. And she said "please, take me out of here." I mean when I saw her, I—first thing I see, like, my grandmother. I mean full of so sadness, and so happy at the same time I discover her. (Eggers 2009a)

This rendition of the encounter bears familiar elements from Zeitoun's interview, with its reference to his grandmother. He also reiterates the ambivalent evaluation at the anecdote's end, with this conclusion that he was "full of so sadness, and so happy at the same time" (Eggers 2009a).

In relating the image that has become the iconic kernel of this narrative, Zeitoun describes the woman's "dress floating 'round her like—like flower or like umbrella, however you going to say it" (Eggers 2009a). He nods to Eggers's word choice of the "flower," but he returns to a less vulnerable and feminine metaphor of his own—"or like umbrella"—evoking an unexpectedness like his earlier version, in which her dress looked like a balloon. Finally, in an equivocating move, Zeitoun concludes, "however you going to say it." This appears to acknowledge Zeitoun's awareness of the differences between his version and that of Eggers, but it also gestures toward dismissing either choice. In keeping with the ambiguity expressed elsewhere in Zeitoun's account, he seems unwilling to endorse Eggers's consistency in portraying him as a hero with a definite purpose.

With the host's explanation, the audience turns "back now to author Dave Eggers," who adds his own narrative evaluation to the story Zeitoun has just told: "Because the canoe was so quiet, he was able to hear things that others weren't. And others going around in motorboats and fan-boats that are so incredibly loud, he was in this quiet canoe and was able to sort of help animals and people and see things and hear things that others weren't able to" (Eggers 2009a). By offering this explanation, Eggers paints Zeitoun's presence as mysterious or even predestined. He is singled out from other survivors and rescuers, as a patient figure moving calmly through the chaos around him. This image resonates with readers and reviewers, who zero in on those events and qualities that form a familiar narrative of heroism.

In an August 2009 review of Zeitoun for the New York Times, Timothy Egan echoes Eggers's heroic tone. Egan writes, "Zeitoun paddles around New Orleans in his canoe for a week, an angel of mercy." He continues, focusing once more on the rescue scene:

Zeitoun saves elderly and dehydrated residents trapped in rotting, collapsing homes: "Help me," comes the voice of an old woman. "Her patterned dress was spread out on the surface of the water like a great floating flower. Her legs dangled below. She was holding on to a bookshelf." In his first day in the canoe,

Zeitoun assists in the rescue of five residents. "He had never felt such urgency and purpose," Eggers writes. "He was needed." (Egan 2009)

Not only is this review noteworthy for its choice to quote the scene that resurfaces time after time in retellings of this tale, but it is also interesting in the way it condenses Eggers's language. In the book, the quote Egan selects about Zeitoun's "urgency and purpose" appears three pages after the description of the woman in the floating dress. In between, the story cuts to the actions of Kathy Zeitoun, who has evacuated to Baton Rouge with the couple's children. In the book's reception, then, both the helplessness of the woman being rescued and the unequivocal purpose of her rescuer are emphasized, combining to forge a familiar heroic tale that audiences recognize and embrace.

This perception of Zeitoun as a heroic character is made explicit in one news article that identifies him, following the legal troubles described in detail below, as a "fallen folk hero" (Galofaro 2013). In Eggers's portrayal of him, and in subsequent circulations of his story, is Zeitoun indeed cast as a folk hero?[9] What are the implications of this role? In the mid twentieth century, heroic figures in folklore were theorized as belonging to a set of universal types: the clever hero, the unpromising hero, the defender or deliverer, the benefactor, the culture hero, and the martyr (Klapp 1949:19). In depicting Zeitoun as a hero, Eggers draws on these universal categories. What Orrin Klapp categorizes as "the deliverer" is perhaps most apparent in Eggers's portrayal: "[D]elivering heroes characteristically come to rescue a person or group from danger or distress" (21). Eggers's emphasis on these "delivering" actions helps Zeitoun emerge in the text (and its subsequent circulation) as a one-dimensional, altruistic character, rather than a complex person doing good deeds with an ambiguous attitude. Klapp notes, in an observation that continues to be relevant despite later challenges to his schema of heroic types, that "[e]ven popular heroes of the present day are subject to a myth-making process" (17) and that "[w]hen a performance [of heroism] attracts the attention of the public, it is apprehended in terms of basic categories. Other roles are then imputed to the hero in consistency with the heroic character" (25). Indeed, as Zeitoun became a known figure through these publications of his story, certain characteristics were attributed to him in keeping with popular conceptions of heroic qualities and actions.

Culturally specific conceptions of heroism, however, belie universal archetypes such as the one invoked by Eggers. Because traditional narratives shared by a particular group express their unique values and beliefs, the qualities depicted as heroic are not equivalent across cultures (Roberts 1990). Furthermore, in contexts where the status quo is challenged, such as disaster, "[f]olk heroic creation as an emergent process is one of the ways by which cultural groups attempt to facilitate adherence to group values during periods of intense change" (Roberts 1990:12). The fashioning of Zeitoun as a folk hero is culturally and contextually specific, then, but it does not reflect the values of Syrian American immigrants, or Muslims, or contractors—or any of the groups with which Zeitoun might conceivably align himself. Rather, it reflects the values of Eggers and others of the contemporary American literary establishment, in a moment at which American values are thrown into question by the aftermath of Katrina. Thus, in drawing on heroic types, Eggers is not drawing on those that are most appropriate culturally or contextually, and the heroic qualities ascribed to Zeitoun are more reflective of those values at which Americans were grasping in the years following Katrina, rather than values which characterize Zeitoun or any group to which he belongs.

The key issue is not that Zeitoun should have been cast in a different static role of an alternative heroic type, but rather that what is seen as heroic is subject to negotiation in any given context. If the final publication of *Zeitoun* had included negotiations between Eggers and Zeitoun about how Zeitoun is characterized in the book, this might have revealed interesting moments of conflict or consensus about heroism, and certainly would have illuminated more of the complexity of Zeitoun and his story. Instead, *Zeitoun* is written and received as an undisputed heroic type—and furthermore, as confirmation that there are heroes and villains in the world and that they are recognizable based on a few predictable behaviors.

Heroism also emerges in public discourse in ways that extend beyond recourse to standard heroic roles. In popular news stories from the early twentieth century to the present day, accounts of "everyday heroism" prevail, documenting and celebrating "heroic acts of people other than uniformed police officers, firemen, and soldiers" (Mechling 1998:41). Jay Mechling argues that such news stories serve to "provide reassuring proof of altruism as a basic instinct that will provide a safety net in a modern society of strangers" (37). Conceptions of heroism, then, are not limited to expressing values commonly enacted by a particular culture, but also those to which a culture aspires—and for which, in the face of evidence to the contrary, they hold out hope.

In the case of Katrina, where first responders were turned away because of misplaced fear and bureaucratic incompetence, everyday heroism took on great importance. Stories about neighbors saving neighbors are shared matter-of-factly by those who endured the storm. But when such actions are reported by community outsiders, taken out of context, and made to fit a mold or type—as in the case of *Zeitoun*—they become something beyond stories of everyday heroism. Perhaps they reflect, in such cases, not only the purpose noted by Mechling, reassurance of an ultimately altruistic human nature, but also the desire to assuage a shared sense of guilt about the absence of heroic responses from outsiders. One subtext of *Zeitoun*, then, might be an insidiously comforting message that Katrina's victims did not need others' help, because they were their own heroes.

This is not a criticism that has been leveled at Eggers by others. On the contrary, Eggers has been praised for the political critiques explicit in *Zeitoun* (Thomas 2012; Lloyd 2014; Keeble 2014). Eggers does, for example, disrupt anti-Muslim stereotypes (Thomas 2012) and productively call attention to disaster-response issues that were often overlooked after 9/11 (Keeble 2014), such as the blurred boundaries between domestic policing and military actions. However, these critics also find in Eggers's text a further, implicit critique; they argue that the "facelessness" of non-white victims (Lloyd 2014) and the "erasure of Blackness" (Thomas 2012) constitute a challenge by Eggers to dominant discourses, a strategic depiction of silences and elisions. These silences can more readily be read, though, as patterns of exclusion, and the most pernicious example is the exclusion of Zeitoun. Despite his seeming centrality and inclusion, Zeitoun's actual participation in the creation of this narrative is rendered invisible in the final, published product—and the result is a character that sheds very little light on the man himself.

Conclusion

In an ironic and disturbing turn of events, the public "character" of Abdulrahman Zeitoun has transformed from valiant to evil. The demand for unambiguous heroism met by Eggers's book finds its inverse in Zeitoun's recent publicity, wherein revelations of domestic abuse have quickly recast him as a villain in the eager public eye. Public circulation of personal narratives tends toward the absolute rather than the ambiguous, so, rather than a continuously complex person, we see a dramatically reversed character—from wrongly imprisoned hero to criminal who should not be on the streets.

As many news outlets reported in August 2012, Zeitoun was arrested twice and sentenced to jail time for assaulting his wife, Kathy. After the first incident, the two were divorced. Zeitoun was then charged with solicited murder, accused of hiring someone to kill his former wife. As the *New York Times* summed up those events, "[t]he couple divorced last year after he was convicted of assaulting her. And on Wednesday [August 8], the New Orleans police charged him with plotting to have Kathy Zeitoun, her son and another man murdered" (Brown 2012). In July 2013, Zeitoun was found not guilty of these charges, and the acquittal was met with public dismay and criticism from Kathy and others. In 2014, Zeitoun was arrested multiple times for violating Kathy's restraining order against him, resulting in various legal consequences, from release due to a legal loophole (May 2014), to electronic monitoring (June 2014), to release by bond (July 2014), to jail without bond (November 2014). In 2016, he was convicted of felony stalking and sentenced to four years in prison.

This story of spousal abuse is unfortunately a familiar one, deserving of investigation in its own right. However, my objective here is not to examine the details of the crimes. Rather, I wish to explore how Zeitoun's narrative of personal experience during Katrina is both implicitly and explicitly invoked in the discourse surrounding his subsequent appearances in the news. Zeitoun's allies have suggested that being a public figure made him unfairly into a target. The *New Orleans Advocate* reported that one of Zeitoun's relatives "blames Eggers' book for foisting undue media attention on his cousin" (Simerman 2014). This defense is not limited to friends and family; the *Times-Picayune* reported that Zeitoun's "attorneys had argued that the district attorney's office had trumped up the charges on their client because of his fame" (Martin 2013).

Other commentators, both journalists and members of the general public, have speculated based on Eggers's story that Zeitoun's traumatic experiences spurred his violent behavior. This line of thought is echoed in some scholarship; A. G. Keeble writes, "One cannot help but wonder if the horrific and traumatic experiences of both Kathy and Abdulrahman, during the aftermath of Katrina, played a role in their marital breakdown, or in Abdulrahman's alleged violence" (2014:187). Rather than trying to determine whether the experiences of Katrina drove Zeitoun to violence, we might ask what the conditions are that allow us to understand both the trauma of Zeitoun's incarceration and the trauma of Kathy's abuse. This demands recognition that trauma is social and public—not an isolated private event, but a vibration or tear in an interconnected web. In the case of Abdulrahman and Kathy, part of that web is a history of abuse, and part of it is Zeitoun's wrongful arrest; the web is connected by the narratives that describe these incidents and others. The narrative of Zeitoun as hero, circulated by Eggers, initially complicated the efforts of Kathy and her attorneys to present another version of Zeitoun, as an abusive spouse. However, the narrative that subsequently took hold, of a Muslim man as always-already criminal, prevents people from seeing Zeitoun's unlawful incarceration during the hurricane as a problem. Zeitoun never fit neatly into either of these narratives, and trying to make him do so is a lose-lose scenario: if he is cast as the hero, the domestic abuse is overshadowed and its allegations received with skepticism; if he is cast as a stereotypical villain, that negates the prevalence of domestic abuse across ethnic and religious groups and discredits the legitimate critique of the institutions that wrongfully imprisoned him during Katrina.

Some members of the public, voicing their opinions via comments on online news sites, have claimed that Zeitoun's behavior is typical of a Muslim male, and thus people should not be surprised by it, despite Eggers's favorable depiction. Such commenters usually go on to associate Zeitoun with all Muslim males and sometimes even a larger, vaguely defined group of immigrants who—according to these commenters—should not be living in the United States. Although many of the vitriolic comments have since been removed from the various articles that reported Zeitoun's crimes, a representative response in this vein reads as follows:

> He comes from a culture/religion of violence and hate, where, after a divorce—
> the woman gets NOTHING, and where beating women you own—is an accepted
> practice, as evidenced by the lack of negative reaction (and indeed the support)
> of the local muslim/arabic populace in New Orleans. I don't see where there is
> anything to be shocked, or surprised about, here. (Albert_F 2012)

This commenter equates Zeitoun's abuse of Kathy with his Muslim religion, based on prevalent American stereotypes associated with Muslim men and women, and admonishes other readers for being astonished after Eggers's hero turned out to be a violent criminal.

Just as Zeitoun's post-Katrina exploits were fitted to a dominant narrative of American heroism, his recent actions are aligned with a different dominant narrative of oppressive Islamic masculinity. Zeitoun has become no more complex or dynamic a character; he is just starring in a different role. What is remarkable about this transition is the ease with which it occurs. Dave Eggers went to extraordinary measures to cast Zeitoun as a hero, countering the discursive contexts of his arrest and imprisonment that cast him as at best suspect and, at worst, a violent proponent of Islamic fundamentalism. It is not merely ironic that this worst-case narrative ends up describing Zeitoun in another context. In part, Eggers's departure from Zeitoun's ambiguity, in his efforts to create a fixed oppositional narrative, ultimately lent authority to the discourse he tried to avoid.

All of these recent engagements with Zeitoun's public persona, whether they are supportive or critical of Zeitoun as an individual, draw heavily on the heroic narrative created by Eggers. Thus, it is not surprising that some critics of *Zeitoun* have called for Eggers to be accountable for misrepresenting

Zeitoun and his relationship with Kathy. A 2012 *Salon* article reports, "When he finished chapters, he'd send them to the Zeitouns for accuracy, and they went over the manuscript 'six or seven' times, leading one to ponder: If you had editorial privilege over your own story, would you whitewash? Would you be tempted to be more heroic, smarter, prettier, kinder, funnier, friendlier, and on and on?" (Patterson 2012). Keeble continues in this vein, questioning Eggers's level of responsibility: "[T]here have been several suggestions that Eggers got Zeitoun wrong, that Eggers may have allowed himself to be seduced or charmed by one side of a complex character" (2014:187). *Zeitoun* certainly only presents one side of a complex character, but not as a result of negligence or deception. Crafting Zeitoun into a less complex, more heroic character was exactly Eggers's intention, and it resulted in the success and popularity of his book. But ultimately, these observations miss the fundamental point that we have no idea what Zeitoun or Eggers did to the story, because that process has been rendered invisible by Eggers's final presentation of the narrative. If those exchanges that took place during the process of production—Zeitoun's objections, Eggers's concessions, and so on—were part of the final product, we would have a much more dynamic version of Zeitoun, and a much more ethical interaction with his story. We would not feel, as Patterson's *Salon* piece implies, duped by our sympathies for an abusive man and, consequently, not dismiss the well-documented injustices that he suffered.

Tracking the variations of Zeitoun's story as it moves from personal experience to public discourse reveals precisely what Guy Beiner identifies as the mystery of social memory: "why certain information was remembered and other information forgotten" (2007:32). The nuances of Zeitoun's character slowly but surely fall away as his story travels, whereas the traits that fit the mold of dominant narratives—whether of the heroic or the villainous—are heightened. In this and in other cases of personal narratives made public, those stories most likely to interrupt dominant discourse are those that opt for complexity over fixity. Unfortunately, though, what becomes "fixed" as public memory is not the complex story; instead, it is the one that sounds most familiar. Disrupting this fixity, and reintroducing complexity, is critical for more ethical commemoration of past disasters and more effective responses to current and future ones. This necessary complexity can be achieved in part by incorporating, within the text itself, the dialogic processes inherent in narrative production.

CHAPTER THREE

Katrina Stories Get Graphic in
A.D.: New Orleans after the Deluge

I n a TED talk, "The Visual Magic of Comics," Scott McCloud remarks that "comics is a kind of call and response in which the artist gives you something to see within the panels, and then gives you something to imagine between the panels" (2005). In *A.D.: New Orleans after the Deluge*, a rendering in comics of Hurricane Katrina, the seen and the imagined combine to form negative stereotypical representations of the storm's survivors. *A.D.* is a non-fiction graphic novel, created by comic artist Josh Neufeld and based on the stories of seven New Orleans residents. The book began as a serially produced web comic, published on the *SMITH Magazine* website.[1] During 2007 and 2008, the online version of *A.D.* was produced, and in 2009, Pantheon Press published it as a book. The narratives in *A.D.*, much like Zeitoun's tale, demonstrate that stories about traumatic experience that "travel" well between the particular and the universal (Shuman 2005), and those that achieve mass appeal in the literary marketplace, are often stories that confirm their readers' preconceptions. Neufeld's choices and his audience's responses reflect the text's implicit claims that fixed, stereotypical identities are representative of cultural and experiential diversity, as well as readers' eagerness to accept that troubling premise.

"Standing In": Selection and Characterization of Categories

Neufeld intended from the start to make *A.D.* a representative sampling of Hurricane Katrina narratives:

> I felt it was important to tell the story from the perspectives of a range of real people who had lived through the storm: well-off and poor, black and white,

young and old, gay and straight, male and female, those who evacuated and those who stayed behind, people who were greatly affected by the flooding and even some who weren't. (2009a:191)

Neufeld's list fixes these categories as oppositional (e.g., "gay and straight"). This belies similarities across categories, and it obscures the intersectionality of these identities (Crenshaw 1991). The underlying principle in Neufeld's book—that putting faces on a checklist of identities translates to equal representation of a diverse, ruptured community—is a faulty one. The presentation of hurricane survivors in *A.D.* upholds negative stereotypes rather than challenging and revising dominant discourses about Katrina.

Neufeld draws real life New Orleanians and depicts their narratives in five chronological sections: "The Storm," "The City," "The Flood," "The Diaspora," and "The Return." The seven people featured are Denise, Leo and his girlfriend Michelle, Abbas and his friend Darnell, Kwame, and Dr. Brobson.² Denise is an African American counselor who rides out the brunt of the storm in her Central City apartment, endures a long wait for rescue first at a local hospital and then at the Convention Center, and struggles financially and emotionally to finally return to New Orleans after two and a half years in Baton Rouge. Leo and Michelle are a young white couple living in Mid-City who evacuate, stay with friends and family around the country, then return about three weeks after the storm to find their apartment and belongings destroyed. Abbas is a middle-aged Iranian man who stays in New Orleans to protect the small supermarket he owns. His friend Darnell, an African American man, stays with Abbas in the store for days until they accept a boat ride out of the city. Abbas returns to New Orleans the week after the storm, and Darnell relocates to Atlanta. Kwame is an African American high school student from New Orleans East who evacuates with his family. Despite finishing high school in California and then attending college in Ohio, Kwame visits New Orleans frequently, where his parents are rebuilding their home and his father's church. Finally, Dr. Brobson is a middle-aged white man who spends the storm in his upscale French Quarter home with his male partner. Brobson hosts friends for a hurricane party, then offers his medical assistance to people around the French Quarter in the weeks following the storm.

Neufeld and Smith, the editor of *SMITH Magazine*, discuss their process of deciding whose stories to feature in *A.D.* in a video titled *Comic Book News and Reviews: Pulp Secret Report*, in May 2007. In the video, Neufeld explains, "[T]here were a couple people that we kinda knew right away that we wanted to use, and the first one was Leo, who's the comic book fan." Leo is a heterosexual white man, not to mention a comic collector, and as such is the character who shares the most—at least in terms of visible attributes—with Neufeld. Mentioning him as their first clear choice perhaps resonates with this book's origins in Neufeld's own story of volunteering with the Red Cross after the storm. If *A.D.* is not to be a narrative about his experiences, it can at least have a character who stands in for him in a way. In fact, Neufeld writes later, in a comment thread on the web version of *A.D.*, "My goal often is to have one character's specific experience—say with evacuating the city, or suffering the effects of the hurricane, or dealing with the flooding—stand in for many of the others, so as to not repeat things too much" (Neufeld 2007–8). Although this has more to do with the arrangement of plot than with the initial selection of characters, it indicates the author's belief that not only is "standing in" possible, it is an effective storytelling strategy. Neufeld operates with the assumption that if we as readers have seen one response to the rising floodwaters, we can imagine the others; similarly, if we have one straight, white, male artist in the story, we can extrapolate and fill in the experiences of other similar individuals.

Certainly, there is a practical necessity for being selective. As Smith acknowledges in their video, "We obviously have a mix of different experiences; some stayed for the hurricane, some got out right away. There's many many more perspectives, but five is about what we could handle" (*Comic Book News and Reviews* 2007). What is interesting here is not the fact of selectivity, but rather the logics behind it, and then the way in which it is read as comprehensive. Authors and publishers, informed by consumers, view the inclusion of multiple identity categories as sufficiently representing a diverse and complete picture of communal trauma. Ultimately, though, their tokenistic approach to multiplicity flattens the experiences of vastly different people and groups. It ignores the intersectionality of people living at the nexus of social constructions and disguises the structural inequality among the categories it portrays.

Scrutinizing these shortcomings in the specific case of Neufeld is also an inquiry into the conditions that make his work possible and popular. In many genres with different authors, publishers, and readers involved, the same kinds of faulty assumptions emerge about multiplicity: if there are enough different types of people, familiar in their reductive categorization, then we can rest easy that we are getting the full story of public disaster. These conventions characterize the production of many texts portraying Katrina, and their results collectively reinforce simplistic misconceptions rather than asking readers to reconsider them. The print version of *A.D.* presents characters whose depictions confirm readers' stereotypes, although the online version of Neufeld's comic initially offered the possibility of disrupting oversimplified representations of Katrina survivors, in that it included critical dialogue in the text's production, circulation, and reception.

"A Big Ol' Po' Boy": Stereotypes in *A.D.*

Darnell's role in the story of *A.D.* and his verbal and visual depictions coincide with persistent racial stereotypes of African American men. He is presented as the exceedingly loyal friend of the storeowner Abbas; despite suffering a great deal from asthma and other afflictions, Darnell insists, "No, Abbas—I told you already. I ain't leavin—(wheeze)—without you" (Neufeld 2009a:131). This paints a picture of Darnell as being "selfless, faithful and deferential" (White and Fuentez 1997:74) against his own best interest. Furthermore, there are many instances where Darnell serves "as amusement object and black buffoon" (74). He is frequently shown as being more interested in eating and drinking than survival, focusing on provisions such as "beef jerky" and "beer" (Neufeld 2009a:88), whereas Abbas makes sure they have practical items for survival such as "flashlights" and a "Red Cross first aid kit" (51). In many panels Darnell is shown eating (64, 84, 89) or sleeping (161), while Abbas is checking the water levels, trying to get in touch with family, or, later, rebuilding his store.

Darnell is clearly an object of humor in "The Flood" section of *A.D.* As the night approaches on August 29, Abbas suggests they try to "get some rest and see how things are later" (90). Standing next to an emptied shelf, he remarks, "I'll sleep here, and you take the sandwich counter" (90), to which Darnell responds, "I know, I know—because I look like a big ol' po' boy!" (90). The subsequent panel shows their joint laughter echoing outside the store, over dark floodwater rising ominously in the street. The same scene appears in chapter 8 of the original webcomic, to which one reader responds, "Thanks for that final chuckle. People need to find humor in the midst of horror" (Neufeld 2007–8). Darnell is doubly the object of humor here; he both makes fun of himself (his size, shape, and affinity for food), and he serves as an ironic example of carelessness in the face of danger that is obvious to others—in this case, the readers of the comic. In depicting Darnell as goofy, lazy, and deferential, Neufeld draws on negative stereotypes associated with black men. In part because of their historical associations, these characterizations are seen as humorous by his audience (Thibodeau 1989).

Furthermore, in terms of visual representation, the classic comics technique of "iconic abstraction" (McCloud 1993:50) backfires when characters such as Darnell are depicted as standing in for oversimplified categories of

DARNELL-- LOOK OUT!

Darnell faces danger in *A.D.: New Orleans after the Deluge,* by Josh Neufeld.

identity. One representation of Darnell, at a dramatic moment when a large piece of furniture almost falls on him, harkens unmistakably to racist carica-tures of black men. His exaggerated lips, wide-open mouth, and bulging eyes are characteristic of the blackface minstrel tradition and racialized cartoons that evolved from it. Because the details upon which Neufeld focuses in draw-ing Darnell refer to a lineage of racist images, the "essential 'meaning'" (30) that gets amplified in this abstraction is the set of characteristics associated with those historical stereotypes. Moreover, the visual depiction of Darnell, like other representations of Katrina survivors, has real world implications. Billy Sothern describes the discovery, shortly before Katrina, of "a hand-made wooden target behind the Jefferson Parish Correctional Center in Gretna. It was cut in the shape of an overweight man, with extra-large white googly eyes, large red lips, and an orange jumpsuit painted on ... [I]t was clear that the target was a caricature of a black man done in the old-fashioned, racist Sambo style" (2007:65). Referring to an incident during Katrina when officials blocked a largely African American group of evacuees from walking out of the flooded city over a bridge into neighboring Gretna, Sothern drives home the point that this racist caricature "is what Jefferson Parish sheriff's depu-ties, who were among the forces that barred the bridge, were using for target practice" (65). Their training made them see the evacuees as inhuman and as potential threats, rather than as people in dire need of help. Visual stereo-types, such as the one that Neufeld reinforces in his representation of Darnell, informed racist behavior by official responders that prolonged the suffering of Katrina's African American victims. While Neufeld would presumably denounce such actions, based on his stated objectives in producing *A.D.* and many of the steps he took to counter negative portrayals of survivors, he nevertheless perpetuates the dominant visual and verbal narratives that fostered such actions in Katrina's wake.

Given depictions such as Darnell's, it is surprising that scholarship on *A.D.* tends to overlook or excuse Neufeld's reliance on stereotypes. Regarding Darnell being cast as the butt of the joke, Jim Coby sees no issue with Neufeld's humorous intent: "[T]he juxtaposition between the 'supplies' which Darnell finds important with those on the checklist should provide a brief respite of humor in the midst of the raging storm. Clearly, these items are totally inadequate for braving a hurricane and beneath these panels Neufeld provides a hyperlink to the National Hurricane Center's hurricane safety checklist," creating a "moment of levity afforded by the contrast between beef jerky and flashlights" (2015:119–20).[3] Coby does not go on to recognize how this humorous juxtaposition pits outsiders who can presume to know better (Neufeld and readers) against the foolish local: the inadequacy portrayed here is affixed to Darnell, and by extension, to African American men in New Orleans who were seen as deserving of the consequences of Katrina because of their own failures.

Some pedagogically oriented researchers find that simplified, recognizable categories effectively represent different groups affected by Katrina, presumably increasing the educational benefits of the text (Schwartz 2010; Siepmann 2015). Other scholars describe the stereotypes that Neufeld deploys and then defend those representational choices. Joseph Donica writes that in representing diverse groups of New Orleanians, "Neufeld's interpretation of those classes fits into the stereotypes that the nation and its political rhetoric often falls back on. His goal is not to stereotype for its own end but to use each character to stand for a part of the population that was affected" (2015:13). Though even this explanation is perplexing—because the ends do not justify the means—Donica takes his argument further: rather than "dismiss [Neufeld's] narrative as reifying racial, gender, and class stereotypes," we should see how he "offers an alternative" (14). This alternative, according to Donica, is in Neufeld's depictions of characters' affective responses to the storm, in the turn some take to activism following Katrina, and in the book's "showing the rupture of the social hierarchy in New Orleans" (14), although he offers no evidence of how this supposed rupture takes place or how it is portrayed in *A.D.* Furthermore, Donica claims that Neufeld's representation "disrupts . . . stereotypes by frustrating the reader's expectations of how his subjects should behave. Denise, the educated social worker, is presented as the chain smoking 'angry black woman'" (13). Here, in his own example of how a stereotype is purportedly disrupted, he illustrates how it is reinforced: despite Denise's real-life credentials and profession, she is reduced in this comic to the role of "angry black woman," an issue that I return to at length below.

Elsewhere, observers either are not able to or refuse to see how Neufeld's representations are stereotypical. Anthony Dyer Hoefer writes that "none of these characters adhere to the stereotypes that populate representations of the city" (2012:296), going on to specify that there are no "voodoo priestesses," "jazz musicians," "Cajun shrimpers," and so on (297). It seems here that Hoefer is referring to popular culture representations, and he is correct in a limited way in observing that some of those touristic and popular images long associated with New Orleans thankfully do not fill the pages of *A.D.* However, *A.D.* is populated by more broad categories represented in stereotypical ways, as in the characterization of the one gay man as an extravagant hedonist, and as in the representations of Darnell and Denise as, respectively, foolish and angry. Hoefer also makes the case that "Neufeld's images and narrative emphasize the particularity of these characters" (320), counteracting their potential to be read as stereotypes or mere representatives of categories. However, the analysis that Hoefer provides to illustrate this point undermines his claim.

Hoefer describes how Neufeld used media images as inspiration and how his revisions of those images show us individuals whose "experiences constitute unique and particular narratives of suffering and injustice" (306). Specifically, he compares Neufeld's drawings to a photograph from the *Times-Picayune* by Ted Jackson, featuring a man holding a baby, with another person behind them, slumped over in a chair. Hoefer shows how the man with the baby was clearly the source image for one of Neufeld's panels, down to the designs on the man's clothes. Hoefer goes on to say that the figure in the chair in Jackson's photograph is "Miss Williams," and that Neufeld altered the original image in positive ways in his text by portraying her later and separately from the man, to emphasize her individuality (306). However, the person in the background in Jackson's picture is a man; although it is not clear whether he is dead or alive, his eyes are closed, and his head leans at an awkward angle on the arm of a lawn chair. His face and body are exposed to the camera. This is not the same person as the woman referred to as "Miss Williams" in *A.D.* That woman, whose real name was Ethel Freeman and whose image in *A.D.* was also inspired by a widely circulated news photograph, sits in profile in a wheelchair, her face and some of her body covered with a poncho.[4] Hoefer's mistake indicates that even careful readers can view the figures in *A.D.* as interchangeable and that they are not in fact shown or perceived as "unique and particular."

In a more convincing and productive thrust of the scholarship on *A.D.*, Hoefer and others describe elements in the webcomic version of the text that engage readers and disrupt harmful, static narratives, although these elements are lost in the transition to the print edition. The webcomic includes interactive features such as hyperlinks, podcasts, and a comments section, which help "compel the reader to more actively and critically approach the public record and the popular memory of post-Katrina New Orleans" (Hoefer 2012:299). These web elements provide a broader context in which to read about the individual lives portrayed, and they enable conversation among readers, Neufeld, and the featured survivors. As Coby notes, "occasionally when inconsistencies would appear, it was the readers who helped correct the mistakes," making *A.D.* "quite literally *about* the people and *by* the people" (2015:121). Neufeld has remarked that reader feedback would let him "find out what's working, what's not working, or what pushes people's buttons and so forth" (*Comic Book News and Reviews* 2007). These kinds of engagement allow the survivors' stories to remain dynamic, avoiding a neat and tidy narrative that "too easily assigns blame on a scapegoat" or "provides its audience with a sense of catharsis that forestalls necessary action" (Hoefer 2012:313). But this relative openness of the web version, including locals' expertise and survivors' commentary, disappears in the printed text. Gone are "the epitexts and peritexts that carry the traces of complex textual histories" (Whitlock and Poletti 2008:x), and in their place, are comic characters who become static stereotypes as they are consumed without the benefit of dynamic contextualization.

"That Woman Is Me": Representativeness Gone Wrong

The comment thread of the webcomic facilitated an especially interesting exchange between a reader and *A.D.*'s Denise,[5] wherein their disagreement illuminates problems with one person standing in for a category of people. Because this conversation is not part of the print comic, that text loses Denise's important critical perspective on the reception of her narrative. The conversation unfolds in the comments on chapter 5, where the final panels portray Denise alone in her apartment at the height of the storm, in the early hours of August 29. In panel 13, she stands—arms and legs splayed for support—in a doorway; walls crumble around her, the building itself seems to buckle in the wavy lines of the floor and ceiling, and wind and rain burst in through a shattered window. The wide-eyed Denise looks stunned. In the subsequent panel, which is divided into two frames, Denise dives onto a bed that she had previously lodged in the hallway for emergency shelter. The first frame shows her full body, suspended in the air over the bed; the second frame is a close-up of her distraught face and her hands clinging to the mattress.

Denise in doorway in *A.D.: New Orleans after the Deluge,* by Josh Neufeld.

Denise on bed in *A.D.: New Orleans after the Deluge,* by Josh Neufeld.

One of the first commenters on this chapter is Dean Haspiel, a relatively well-known comic artist and former collaborator with Neufeld. Dean writes, "A.D. continues to amaze as Josh pits reportage with art and makes universal fiction with emotional truths" (Neufeld 2007–8). Given the nonfiction status of the text, it is unclear at first what Dean means by "universal fiction." He continues, "My only criticism is with the last panel when the woman screams 'I'm gonna die in this bitch!' It felt forced and took me out of the drama" (Neufeld 2007–8). With this criticism, it becomes clearer that Dean finds this to be a story that can have universal resonance, one that can be true in ways to everyone. Because this moment feels dissonant for him, it breaks the otherwise sustained "fiction" that makes the reader feel present in the experience. Dean explains exactly what takes him "out of the drama" of Denise's near-death experience:

> I could almost hear the gangsta drum beats behind her "rap" and wondered if she really blurted that line when she was alone and scared with her cat in the confines of her compromised position? I have faced many awful situations and discovered that my faux bravado diminishes greatly when I think I'm about to perish. Still, if that's how it went down, I'm impressed! (Neufeld 2007–8)

Dean does not find Denise's reaction realistic, partly because her response is not what he imagines his own would be. Additionally, it reminds him too much of a particular genre—rap music—that he thinks is an inappropriate mode of expression in this instance.

Almost immediately (seven hours later, according to the comments' time stamps), Denise herself responds to Dean in this way:

> Dean, [t]hat woman is me, and that is exactly what I was thinking at that moment and for many, many moments during the hurricane. I was terrified, and that was my expression of terror, not false bravado. And maybe, just maybe, rap music reflects the very real language of a very real people. Because, frankly, I talked like that before I ever heard a rap record. (Neufeld 2007–8)

Remarkably, the comment forum of the webcomic allows Denise to confront Dean directly about his misreading of her speech. Her first sentence alone collapses his fragile construction of a "universal fiction," because "that woman" whom Dean is reading as a character in a story, as Denise succinctly puts it, "is me." Denise also addresses Dean's other misconception: where he projected false bravado, Denise points out her terror. Finally, Denise takes on Dean's criticism of what he hears as the misplaced sounds of rap music.

To Denise's corrections, Dean replies: "Hey, Denise—Fair enough. I grew up on the origins of hip-hop in the upper west side of Manhattan and I cherish the music. Just ask Josh" (Neufeld 2007–8). With this reach for credibility, Dean seeks to establish his own right to critique rap, which really is not the crux of the debate between these two. Rather, it appears to be a slightly muted battle over who has the right to say what is appropriate in terms of a realistic representation of an African American woman. Whereas Dean finds Denise's language too much like rap, and therefore removed from reality,

Denise counters that the language of rap is part of her reality. With this, Dean promptly backpedals and claims it as part of his reality, too. Dean goes on to justify his criticism:

> Still, there are some things that happen in real life that don't always translate well in adaptation, especially in semi-autobiographical "fiction," and, for some reason, that very real line of expression [of yours] took me OUT of the drama. I've produced many semi-autobio comix and I find myself editing certain facts so I can get to the meat of the truth better for universal consumption. (Neufeld 2007–8)

Here, Dean gets to the heart of an issue with which many nonfiction texts about Katrina wrestle: the problem of depicting reality versus creating the feeling of reality for "universal consumption" by audiences. What Dean and other critics neglect to address is what kinds of realities *do* translate well, for whom, and at what cost.

Josh Neufeld responds to this conversation on the comment thread, writing, "Dean and Denise, [y]our exchange was fascinating to me, and in a way I can understand both your points. Certainly, as I was writing the scene, I wouldn't have had the Denise character say what she did" (Neufeld 2007–8). He agrees with Dean to an extent; this exclamation does not fit into his expectation about what a near death experience would look and sound like. Neufeld continues: "But I have the benefit of having the actual Denise for inspiration! When Denise told me the 'I'm gonna die in this bitch' line, I just knew I had to use it. I realize that it may take some readers 'out of the story,' but at least in this case, I think it is more important to tell what really happened" (Neufeld 2007–8). He closes by thanking them both and expressing gratitude for Denise's willingness to share the experience in the first place. Although Neufeld seems to be arguing against Dean by insisting on representing the moment as Denise remembers it, interesting qualifications emerge. He recalls that he "just knew [he] had to use" the line in question and concludes that "at least in this case" her reality was the best version of the story to go with. Dean and Josh's disagreement is not really about whether personal stories should be adapted to make them ring true with audiences; it is about which elements of a particular story are most likely to have that effect. Denise's line, then, is a point of contention regarding the believability of Denise's character. Neufeld walks a fine line between making characters seem real to readers and making them into recognizable types. When it comes to depicting Denise, he crosses into the realm of the stereotype.

Early in the process of web publication, Neufeld gave an interview, along with Leo and Denise, in which the three discuss the problems of representing real people in a graphic narrative. While Leo is quite pleased with his incarnation as a comics character, Denise expresses her reservations. She explains:

> Josh and I talked on the front end, and I was kind of critical about the way my character could possibly be perceived. It seemed to me that my character will fall easily into stereotype and I was upset about it. But what I liked was that Josh didn't have a knee-jerk reaction to my criticism. And instead of becoming defensive, he listened to my concerns and he allowed me greater involvement in the process. So right now, I'm really pleased with how things are going. ("Post-Katrina Depicted in Comic Strips" 2007)

Denise is savvy about the dangers of representativeness as well as the pitfalls of the comics form. She knows that certain characteristics will be exaggerated and that she will be read as standing in for the experiences of other African American women.

Josh responds to Denise's expression of concern with the following explanation of how he amended his creative process: "Denise, after she saw her representation in the first chapter, where I sort of introduced the character, she, you know, very rightfully had concern about being portrayed in sort of the stereotypical way of an African-American woman.... [W]e agreed that for future episodes, it just works better all around, I would show her the script before" ("Post-Katrina Depicted in Comic Strips" 2007). The sensitivity that Neufeld displays toward this issue, as well as his willingness to have Denise review and critique his representation of her, is compelling evidence of his artistic responsibility. Nevertheless, the reception of the text by Denise and readers implies that the problem of stereotypical representation is not resolved.

When Neufeld is asked to specify what Denise did not like about how she appeared in the comic, he explains:

> Her first appearance in the book, I guess she came across as caustic or foul-mouthed. Negative, in a knee-jerk way. She thought that was a stereotypical portrayal. I think she called it "an angry black bitch." I could see it from her point of view. She said, "I went through a major trauma, and the person that you know now, who you met after Hurricane Katrina, is a very different person than before Hurricane Katrina." (Neufeld 2009c)

The section of the comic to which Neufeld refers here is really just a glimpse of an introduction to Denise, and the emotions she displays are mild in comparison to later segments in the story. Specifically, her mother shares that she will ride out the hurricane at her workplace, Baptist Memorial Hospital, and

Denise voices skepticism in *A.D.: New Orleans after the Deluge,* by Josh Neufeld.

that the hospital has promised to provide them with a private room for shelter; to this, Denise responds with a smirk, "Yeah, I'll believe that shit when I see it" (Neufeld 2007–8). This panel remains unchanged in the print version of the comic.

Denise's critique of Neufeld, especially regarding how she is portrayed after undergoing trauma, also serves to critique a broader tendency. Many people viewing media coverage of Katrina interpreted the ruptured lives on display as *un*ruptured—they read despair retroactively onto the lives of those seen suffering. This practice was highly visible in former first lady Barbara Bush's remark about survivors in the Houston Astrodome: according to a *New York Times* article from September 7, 2005, Mrs. Bush "declared [the response to Katrina] a success for evacuees who 'were underprivileged anyway,' saying on Monday that many of the poor people she had seen while touring a Houston relocation site were faring better than before the storm hit" ("Barbara Bush Calls Evacuees Better Off"). However, this kind of perception was more widespread than just its instantiation in Mrs. Bush's well-known words: "[T]he way in which the black poor were framed by the media in the days that followed the levee breaches undoubtedly did conform to the race-based assumptions of many viewers" (Hartnell 2010:307). Thus, commonly held—though perhaps not commonly discussed or admitted—stereotypes, in combination with the images circulated by the news media, resulted in "the media in essence provid[ing] a comfortable answer to the uncomfortable revelations about race and class that Katrina uncovered: poor blacks themselves were culpable for their own need" (307). In the process of producing *A.D.*, Denise is well aware of the consequences of feeding the American public the kinds of images it unfortunately expects to see. She knows there is a very real risk that the effects of traumatic experience will be interpreted as the status quo of a frequently misrepresented group of people. Therefore, even though her experience of Katrina was characterized by understandable anger, she is reluctant for that emotion to be highlighted in her graphic incarnation in *A.D.*

Although he is perhaps not as sharply aware of this risk as Denise is, especially at the outset of the project, Neufeld does share her concerns: "I was trying to be very sensitive in my drawings. I didn't want to create stereotypical images of 'scared black faces' or 'angry black faces' or anything like that. There's such a history in comics of stereotypical presentations of black people" (Neufeld 2009b). Here Neufeld demonstrates his awareness both of common stereotypes attached to portrayals of African Americans, and of the particular tradition of those portrayals in the comic form. Why, then, is it so hard for him to avoid re-creating these stereotypes in some ways? Even with Neufeld's sensitivity to the lineage of racism in cartoon images of African American people, and even with Denise's cautions about the particular traps of depicting an angry black woman, the text's audience is still primed to read it in a certain way. The angry stereotype and the racially derogatory comic are both so recognizable that any hint of either spells trouble, and their combination is doomed to a certain extent. These intertwined histories of representation predetermine the character of Denise to the point where her legitimate anger as a survivor of disaster and injustice cannot be read *only* as her anger. The production of a text that selects her as a symbol of a larger category combined with a reader reception saturated in the discourses of black femininity and the traditions of the comics form ensure that her image is read a certain way, informed by stereotypes. Either she confirms them, as in her own concerns about how she appears, or readers find her unbelievable when she does not, as in Dean Haspiel's interpretation of her "terror" in the midst of the storm as hip-hop "bravado." The most telling result of that interaction is that instead of acknowledging that he had misread her emotions, the reader concluded that the moment "took him out of the drama," thereby disrupting the story's appeal for "universal consumption." Stereotypes are easiest to digest when they do not talk back.

How, then, is an artist to avoid the visual history of racist stereotypes, especially when representing, for example, the true story of a black man who approaches danger with a sense of humor, or of a black woman who is angered by injustice? The problem does not lie in asking whether stereotypical qualities are accurate in characterizing real individuals. The problem is that these features are in part what makes stories like these travel from the particular—a traumatized woman is angered by the failure of officials to rescue and aid in the recovery of her and her family—to the (stereotype-informed) universal: black women are angry.

The way out of stereotypical representations is not by thinking they can be avoided—here we see Neufeld's sincere attempts with Denise fail—but by redefining perceived weaknesses as strengths, with the recognition that they are cast as weaknesses because they threaten dominant groups (Collins 1986). In the case of Denise, this redefinition might have come with a contextualized depiction of her anger as circumstantial, rather than as an inherent character trait. Her anger might also have been shown as an effective and appropriate tool in the context of disaster, just as Darnell's humor might have been. In part, this could have been achieved by presenting survivors' narratives in their entirety, rather than fragmenting them. Just as with Zeitoun's story in *Voices from the Storm*, breaking up individual narratives results in reductive snippets, removed from their contexts of production and unable to represent the complexity of their narrators. Finally, Neufeld could have more critically illustrated those powerful structures that make responses such as anger and humor, especially when they are used by African Americans and aligned with historical stereotypes, seem inappropriate and ineffective.

Conclusion

Authors and artists such as Josh Neufeld have an opportunity to redefine stereotypes, resist simplistic identity categorization, and challenge dominant narratives that characterize Katrina and other disasters. It is an opportunity lost in *A.D.: New Orleans after the Deluge*, especially in its print version. The character types who end up on the pages of *A.D.* do not unsettle readers to the point of disrupting official discourse about Katrina. Their characterizations perpetuate stereotypes, and in doing so they fail to redefine those qualities, such as humor and anger, which might have been seen as survival tactics rather than as confirmation of negative associations with generalized categories. This failure is not unique to *A.D.* or to comics, although because a trademark of this genre is simplification and emphasis on iconic features (McCloud 1993), comics foreground this trend that is not as immediately visible in other genres. Moving away from tokenistic representation would make a substantial difference: when publishers and authors are not compelled to take a "one of each" approach to diversity, they do not face the same kinds of challenges and fall into the same kinds of shortcomings. Texts depicting communities in crisis can focus instead on the complexities of an individual life or on the richness of experience in one self-defined group. More generally, though, the key to ethical presentation of survivors' stories in *A.D.* is incorporating their voices—as they comment on their stories' production, circulation, and reception—in the final published product. This inclusion is what allows for rich moments of dialogue on the webcomic version of *A.D.* That dialogue would be even more powerful if it included other voices, such as Darnell's, and if its critical nature had influenced and been incorporated in Neufeld's representations as the comic progressed and transitioned to print.

In a foreword to *Creating Comics as Journalism, Memoir & Nonfiction*, Josh Neufeld writes of comics that "[t]he medium's unique combination of pictures and text and the fragmented narrative of the panel-by-panel format engage the reader in a particularly active role of interpretation and inference" (2016). Other scholars have made a similar case, that because comics make interpretive demands on the reader, they have the potential to be a more ethical form, particularly suited for depicting traumatic narratives (Hirsch 2004; Whitlock 2006; Chute 2008). There are no guarantees, however, about the kind of interpretations to which this form will lead readers. In fact, if readers are being asked to close narrative gaps with what they already know, this seems a particularly likely place for the surfacing of familiar discourses, including harmful stereotypes. In order to prevent the continued circulation of such dominant narratives, then, it is not sufficient to disrupt the medium; authors must also disrupt the message. One way to do this is to incorporate the varied, even critical, input of those to whom the message refers. Otherwise, we are left with texts that do not amplify, as intended, but rather muffle and distort voices such as that of Denise—who, when Neufeld published a tenth anniversary "Where are they now?" comic, "chose not to be interviewed for [the] piece."[6]

Just as with *Trouble the Water*, the documentary described in the following chapter, the verbal and visual rhetoric in *A.D.* succumbs at points to the all too familiar discourse of stereotypes. Also, as with that film, there are moments when such discourse is productively ruptured. In both cases, those moments involve the people whose personal stories are on display questioning or otherwise taking ownership of the process of presentation. These moments are uncomfortable—as illustrated by Dean Haspiel's virtual squirming—but that is as it should be. The intersectionality of identities in communities affected by disaster, as well as the empathic unsettlement that characterizes ethical engagement with depictions of trauma (LaCapra 2001), forestalls reifying representations and neatly wrapped-up narratives. This messiness of identity and of experience in postdisaster lives should not be edited out or resolved for the sake of "universal consumption"; on the contrary, it should be front and center when disaster stories go public.

"They Probably Got Us All on the News": Unsettled Filming in *Trouble the Water*

Tia Lessin and Carl Deal's 2008 documentary *Trouble the Water* features the personal narratives of Katrina survivor Kimberly Roberts, her husband Scott, and their friends and family. The Robertses, an African American family who lived in New Orleans's Ninth Ward prior to Katrina, rode out the hurricane in their flooded home. They fled to a neighbor's home as conditions worsened, and after being forcefully turned away from a local navy base where they sought shelter, they found refuge in a nearby school building. Later, with twenty-five other survivors, they drove a truck to their family's property in Alexandria, Louisiana, where they continued to suffer with no water, no electricity, and delayed emergency aid. They received some assistance at a shelter in Alexandria before Kim, Scott, and their friend Brian were forced further north by Hurricane Rita, which hit Louisiana in September 2005. After residing with family members in Memphis, Kim and Scott finally returned to New Orleans and began rebuilding their lives. *Trouble the Water* relies on traditional documentary techniques such as archival news footage, on-screen text, and direct address to the camera by the film's subjects. However, this film also incorporates footage shot on a handheld camera by Kim Roberts during the hurricane. Incorporating the subject's viewpoint in this way foregrounds the "cracks and tears" necessary for ethical representations of traumatic experience (van Alphen 1997:37).

The Robertses' on-screen engagement with the process of *Trouble the Water*'s production suggests that this film escapes the pattern of delivering comfortably consumable eyewitness narratives of trauma. Like Denise in *A.D.*, these documentary subjects talk back, but unlike her voice, their voices are incorporated into the text in question. Similar to Shawn and Patrice, the SKRH interviewees, the survivors in the film reveal an awareness of their audience's expectations that is both powerful and unsettling. Denise is concerned that audiences will read her emotions in terms of a racist stereotype, Shawn and Patrice know they are competing with dominant narratives portraying them as irresponsible, and Kim Roberts expects that "some white folks" will be interested in her footage. When listeners, readers, and viewers are confronted with these implicit characterizations of themselves, they are no longer innocent bystanders; they are made complicit in the suffering that these texts convey. The ethical representation of trauma narratives depends on the resulting uneasiness, and *Trouble the Water* provides a model of how to responsibly integrate this kind of discomfort into a text. However, this film also indulges in a concluding narrative of redemption with respect to Kim and Scott Roberts. As with *Zeitoun*, the established, recognizable storyline lurks behind what is presented as an exceptional particularity. The film's final nod to a dominant narrative of racial uplift, which may ultimately be responsible for the film's public success,[1] appeases audiences troubled by the film's more uncomfortable moments.

Breaking the Frame: *Trouble the Water*'s Unconventional Footage

Right from the start, Lessin and Deal reveal how the film they set out to make was challenged by the reality they encountered; they establish a framework in which preconceptions about Katrina survivors are revised by the survivors themselves. *Trouble the Water* did not begin as a documentary about the Roberts family. In contrast to *A.D.*, where the author and publisher sought out representatives of the categories they wished to portray, the directors/producers of *Trouble the Water* were on an entirely different mission when they first met Kim and Scott. As they put it, "[w]hen we arrived in Louisiana a week after the levees failed, we wanted to tell a different story" (Lessin and Deal). The pair, who had worked together previously as producers on Michael Moore's *Bowling for Columbine* and *Fahrenheit 9/11*, were headed to Louisiana to film the homecoming of Louisiana National Guard troops in the midst of Katrina's aftermath. The military officials on site prevented them from achieving that goal, and they ended up interviewing evacuees at a nearby emergency shelter, coincidentally the same shelter in Alexandria, Louisiana, where Kim and Scott were seeking assistance.

In an early scene in *Trouble the Water*, the filmmakers are in the middle of conducting an interview with someone at the shelter. Just moments into this conversation, Kim and Scott appear for the first time, announcing that they have hurricane footage. Kim's appearance on camera is sudden and confusing, as she begins speaking while the camera is not on her, and the camera operator seems unsure about whether to focus on her while she contends: "This need to be worldwide. All the footage that I seen on TV? Nobody ain't got what I got. I got right there *in* the hurricane." Shortly after this dramatic entrance into the film, *Trouble the Water* cuts to Kim's handheld camera footage, affirming her claims and realizing her declaration that her images, now incorporated in an award-winning and widely circulated documentary film, "need to be worldwide."

Lessin and Deal's inclusion of the scene in which they first meet Kim quickly fills the audience in on how the film became centered on her, but it also sets up an unsettling relationship between Kim, the directors/producers, and the audience. This is different from *A.D.* or *Zeitoun*, where the audience is given the impression that there were no conflicts involved in the selection of subjects, and they are free to feel like conscientious consumers of these narratives. Viewers of *Trouble the Water* are taken aback, along with the camera's lens, by the force of Kim's entry into the visual and auditory frame: immediately they see the power of her presence and her insistence on sharing her story. By opening with this scene, Lessin and Deal expose their own surprise and flexibility, rather than emphasizing directorial control over the subjects of their film. This opening scene is the first of several where Kim asserts her awareness of her testimony's value and the likelihood of its circulation in ways that may make audiences uncomfortable. Kim's footage reveals Katrina survivors' understanding of the discourses with which their stories must contend, and it illustrates the capacity of truth-telling genres to challenge those discourses by foregrounding survivors' engagements with them.

When the documentary cuts to Kim's recording, viewers are quickly immersed in her pre-Katrina life. She walks and bikes through her Ninth Ward neighborhood, narrating over shaky images and occasionally posing questions to people she sees. Given audiences' knowledge of what is to come, these images and interviews take on a nostalgic and tragic quality, such as when a group of young children playfully tell Kim's camera that they are not scared of any hurricane and reveal that their families do not plan to evacuate. Despite those moments of innocence about what the storm will bring, Kim repeatedly asserts her cognizance of what she is documenting and why. She remarks that she is taking her "before and after shots" and that she will continue to capture "live and direct footage when this here go down." Kim is not an accidental witness to the events of Katrina, a bystander who just happened to have a camera. Rather, she intentionally set out to record what she anticipated would be a historical moment.

Furthermore, Kim's on-camera comments disclose her motivations for creating this record and her expectations about who might be interested in it. She remarks, over the images of her streets and neighbors, "Just in case it's all gone I got it on tape, see? I'm showing the world that we did have a world, before the storm." This declaration eerily anticipates both the destruction of the areas she is filming and the post-Katrina discourse that constructed communities like hers as not having "a world" worth rebuilding.[2] Kim also predicts the following, in conversation with a group of neighborhood women sitting on their front steps: "Right here gonna be a day to remember, that's why I'm recording. Hey and, this thing really hit us, you know, I'll be have something to show my children. If I get some [inaudible] shit, I might could sell it to them white folks, y'all heard me?" In this commentary Kim identifies two potential audiences for her footage, her future children[3] and "them white folks." It is in fact a pair of white film producers who eventually incorporate Kim's footage into their documentary (and, as Kim has joked regarding her trip to Sundance, primarily white audiences at the film festival).[4] This prediction in the documentary is potentially unsettling to viewers: it creates the sensation that Kim is watching them, just as they are watching her. She has already imagined this audience, summoned by the "white folks" who picked up her story and delivered it to them. Does that mean viewers have been manipulated, duped? Does it mean they are participating in an exploitative market, trading in stories of personal struggle? The questions raised by this moment have the power to make viewers—especially white ones—consider the implications of their own viewership, of their own identity in relation to the identity of the film's subjects.

The powerful turning of the spectatorial gaze back on the film's audience is one of this documentary's greatest strengths and a strategy for circulating narratives of traumatic experience that models what Dominick LaCapra calls "empathic unsettlement":

> Historical trauma is specific, and not everyone is subject to it or entitled to the subject position associated with it. It is dubious to identify with the victim to the point of making oneself a surrogate victim who has a right to the victim's voice or subject position. The role of empathy and empathic unsettlement in the attentive secondary witness does not entail this identity; it involves a kind of virtual experience through which one puts oneself in the other's position while recognizing the difference of that position and hence not taking the other's place. (2001:78)

LaCapra argues for a respect for difference that must be achieved by maintaining distance. In part, this is a response to an approach to studying and representing trauma that allows the appropriation of victims' voices and experiences, and as a result, their continuous victimization even by those who mean well.

Empathic unsettlement can be a corrective to what some theorists recognize as a flawed system for the public reception of personal trauma narratives. Gillian Whitlock explains the shortcomings of audience empathy as follows:

> Empathy is attractive, but there is something self-reflective about it, and because empathy makes us feel good, it is very easy to bear ... A more difficult contract for dealing with trauma but a more timely one given "compassion fatigue" might ... complicate the notion that we can assimilate strangers and negotiate difference through empathic understanding. It could, for example, project intractable difference that must be negotiated in other ways. (2007:156; see also Berlant 2004)

Similar to LaCapra, Whitlock insists on the recognition of difference between the speaking subject and the listening one. Identification on the part of the listener not only usurps the place of the narrator; it also precludes the listener from an ethical response. Empathy acts as an anesthetic for the secondary trauma of listening. The uncomfortable alternative, where "the audience is shaken out of complacency," is empathic unsettlement (Hesford 2011:90). In narratives that have this effect, empathy is more likely to become a means to an end—compelling audiences to action—than the end in itself. Furthermore, by discouraging identification with victims, empathic unsettlement creates a communicative context in which audiences can see their own complicity in suffering. These are the powerful effects of the unsettling moments in *Trouble the Water*; audiences are reminded of the "intractable difference" between their position as viewers of this film and Kim's position as survivor and documentarian, and as a result they are forced to consider how their spectatorship—in relation to this and other representations of disaster—implicates them in the discursive and material violence afflicting survivors.

As the film progresses, viewers see Kim's footage of the storm and ensuing flood. Meanwhile, the audience is following the interwoven story of the Robertses in the weeks after the storm, now in the company of Lessin and Deal. The filmmakers also include clips from news coverage of the storm and aftermath, which remind audiences of the external perspective on these events. The news clips sometimes create an ironic contrast with the firsthand footage from Kim's camera. In the chaotic midst of water rushing through Kim's streets—overtopping a stop sign at the intersection outside of her house, where survivors are huddled in the hot, dark attic—the film cuts quickly to a broadcast of then FEMA director Michael Brown, calmly reassuring his interviewer and the news-watching public that FEMA is prepared to respond to this disaster. This juxtaposition critiques the federal government's preparedness for and response to Katrina's flooding.

With good reason, Michael Brown is a popular scapegoat for the mismanagement of responses to Katrina; however, the film's subtler and potentially less popular critiques target the broader American public who watched the news coverage, sometimes accepting the narrative that African American New Orleanians were lawless and violent, and sometimes seeing survivors as helpless victims for whom they felt empathy but not an ethical imperative to respond. One such critique emerges in a scene a little over half an hour into the film. As Kim, Scott, and their neighbors endure their wait in the attic of a flooded home, they watch the water and skies outside through a small dormer window, commenting on the surprising absence of rescuers. At one point, an unnamed woman in the attic with Kim observes, "New Orleans looks dead like a motherfucker. They probably got us all on the news." The film immediately cuts to news coverage of Katrina survivors, confirming the woman's suspicions. In these replayed news broadcasts, viewers of *Trouble the Water* see images that are most likely familiar because they were so widely circulated during the height of the storm's media coverage. There are young African American survivors on a rooftop with scrawled messages pleading for help, and families crowded onto highway overpasses around the city. The familiarity of these images is disconcerting following the astute observation made by Kim's friend. Seeing this coverage again, recontextualized, makes viewers see it differently. Hearing people realize how their suffering is being broadcast, but not alleviated, implicates those who witnessed that suffering from a safe distance.[5] By presenting Kim's firsthand footage in this context, the filmmakers refuse to allow identification and appropriation of the traumatic experiences she and her friends endured. Instead, they reintroduce that intractable distance between the trauma survivor and the audience by reminding viewers what they were likely doing when this happened—standing by and watching.

The filmmakers also incorporate an unusual "double filming" throughout *Trouble the Water*. Although Kim's original footage depicts her experiences before and during the storm, this comes almost entirely to an end once Kim joins forces with Lessin and Deal.[6] Even though there are flashbacks in the film's chronology, they mostly predate the meeting of the Roberts family with the directors/producers. Following this encounter, the professional film crew documents Kim and Scott's struggles. What is striking about this, though, is that Kim continues to use her camera, as does their friend Brian. As a result, there are many points where the viewer is watching Kim or Brian as they record things, but never seeing what they are recording; at times, the audience's inability to see what Kim and Brian see creates the distance necessary for empathic unsettlement.

Kim's continued use of her camera asserts her right and ability to record her experiences, but at the same time, her documentary project has been subsumed by that of Lessin and Deal. As Kim, Scott, and Brian drive into New Orleans with Lessin and Deal for their first post-Katrina visit, viewers get multiple perspectives from within their van. The scene begins with a close shot of Kim talking on the phone, explaining to someone how she survived and is headed back to New Orleans with "some people [she] met." Kim explains, "They doing a documentary. Like a *real* documentary? Like, you know, on . . . hurricanes and stuff." Hearing Kim describe the project in this way reveals her belief that the project of Lessin and Deal bears legitimacy that her own filming did not. Rather than cite their experience, equipment, budget, or any other qualifications, however, Kim refers to their broad topic of "hurricanes." Despite the filmmakers' clear interest up to this point in the Roberts family's experiences, this description hints at Kim's assumption that a documentary would require a topic of more general interest and importance than her own personal story.[7] Nonetheless, Kim follows immediately on that remark by saying, "All in the same minute, I'm teaching Brian how to be a director." Sure enough, the footage from the inside of the van includes images both of the official film crew and of Brian holding a camera. The viewers are left to assume that the shots of the crew are taken by Brian, and vice versa. In this brief scene, then, there is shared authority of directorial control and of visual perspective: we hear Kim say she is with a "real" documentary crew, and we see Brian's viewpoint of them; and then we hear Kim say she is making Brian into a director, and we see the film crew's gaze turned back on him. Finally, Kim has the video camera back, and the audience's view now includes Kim's face, the viewfinding screen of her handheld camera, and the scene of devastation outside the car window. Ironically, Scott remarks at this moment (resonating with the SKRH narratives discussed in chapter 1), "This look like a movie, man. This can't be real."

What are viewers to make of these layered representations, of people filming people, who are simultaneously filming something that looks "like a movie"? The resulting confusion mimics the complicated struggle to depict narratives of traumatic experience. Eyewitness accounts of survivors are often framed and circulated by someone else in attempts to lend them legitimacy, and this framing echoes the survivors' own attempts to record and make sense of surreal experience. Furthermore, survivors are capable of negotiating that external framework, turning it back on itself in order to assert their own authority as producers of narratives. By incorporating this negotiation in *Trouble the Water*, Lessin and Deal challenge the dominant discourse of trauma victims, especially in the case of Katrina, as passive or helpless, and of their stories as ones that can be easily packaged and purchased by consumers eager to feel good about their own capacity for empathy.

While the scenes where viewers see what Kim and Brian are filming are complex and interesting, an even more powerful moment arises when audiences are denied access to the amateur footage, and thus to the survivors' perspective. Upon returning to their Ninth Ward neighborhood, the Robertses and Brian are shocked not only by the destruction, but also by the evidence that few rescuers have been in the area. They read the spray paint markings on homes,[8] noting that in many cases either no one has entered these buildings— at this point, two weeks after the storm—or that the only organization that has searched a home is the local animal rescue team, the LASPCA. Kim's mounting anger culminates when she realizes, "I betcha ... my uncle still in the house, y'all." With this, the group approaches the home where Kim suspects her uncle may have taken shelter during the flood. She dons a surgical mask to protect against odors and toxins, and Brian follows her through the home's front door with the video camera in hand. Viewers see the film crew's perspective, looking in from the front door as Kim and Brian enter a second room. We watch Brian's back in this interior doorway; he films something we cannot see as Kim's voice comes from within the inner room: "Yeah, he been decomposing right here." With this graphic verbal description, we see Brian turn quickly, remarking, "Oh Jesus," and leaving the house with an expression of disgust. Kim confirms, "Yeah, he died up in here, ya heard me?" Based on Kim's narration and Brian's reaction, viewers of *Trouble the Water* have no doubt about what they have found inside the house: the dead body of Kim's uncle, undiscovered by officials and left to rot in the Louisiana heat. However, while Kim and Brian see this horror, we do not. This moment is perhaps the film's most compelling example of empathic unsettlement. As secondary witnesses to this trauma, we are never going to see exactly what they saw. Nor should we, the filmmakers seem to imply. Between what Kim and Brian experienced and what we are able to comprehend, there is an irreconcilable distance that the film, in not exposing that awful image of death, insists on maintaining.

Uplift and Appeasement: *Trouble the Water*'s Conventional Ending

Despite being effectively uncomfortable at many key moments, *Trouble the Water* offers a relatively feel-good conclusion that reinforces dominant narratives rather than continuing to challenge them. First, Scott and Kim are shown happily at work in their respective post-Katrina jobs, then several captions appear to inform viewers of some ongoing issues with the city's recovery, and finally, Kim is shown celebrating with other New Orleanians at a demonstration in front of City Hall. Overall, this resolution lets audiences off the hook too easily, implying not only that Kim and Scott have found closure after their traumatic experiences, but also that these experiences were ultimately positive ones for the couple. Despite paying lip service to locals' uphill battle of recovery, the film's ending is contrary to the insistence, on the part of many hurricane survivors, including Kim Roberts, that the suffering they endured during Katrina is continuous, in both material and emotional terms. Furthermore, ending Kim and Scott's story on an optimistic note relieves the productive tension established by the film's earlier strategies of empathic unsettlement. Instead of feeling implicated by their own passive viewership of enduring hardship, by the end of the film, audiences are left feeling assured that everything worked out for the best.

As the documentary moves toward its problematic conclusion, a caption informs audiences that this final footage is from "six months later" (eighteen months after Katrina hit). The scene opens on a clean, bright New Orleans, complete with sunny, blue skies, in dramatic contrast with the previous scene, which had been filmed at night. The camera cuts to Scott Roberts, who confidently measures and marks a piece of wood in the midst of a construction site. The following sequence reveals that Scott is now doing carpentry, working with "a cool boss" on rebuilding local houses. As he saws wood under the guidance of his employer, Scott's voiceover proclaims, "I ain't got to be looking over my shoulder. I ain't got to be worrying about somebody looking for me with a gun." His lifestyle as it is shown in these closing scenes contrasts with earlier references in the film to his involvement with dealing drugs. In explaining how he came to hire Scott, the older, white man explains that he overheard Scott say, "All I really want to do is work" and concluded, "That's the kind of guy ... you know you can rely on." As the camera shows Scott engaged in physical labor, his voice continues to explain how he feels about this job: "I'm happy I did come back 'cause now I get to rebuild my city ... I come in in the morning, jump straight to work. I love the smell of that sawdust." This final depiction of Scott's post-Katrina life ends with some motivational words he offers to other survivors: "Try to make a difference in your neighborhood if you can't make a difference nowhere else."

In their choice to conclude the documentary in this manner, the filmmakers fall back on the dominant narrative of "racial uplift," specifically as that term refers to the industrial educational philosophies of Booker T. Washington and others in the late nineteenth century. Washington's Tuskegee Institute, perhaps the most well-known manifestation of this belief system, "emphasized manual training, sought to inculcate the dignity of labor, taught a curriculum of rudimentary education, and was intended to produce common-school teachers who would, to the benefit of southern black farmers and their families, inculcate habits of industry, thrift, and morality" (Gaines 1996:34). The conclusion of *Trouble the Water* reflects this narrative in its uncritical celebration of Scott Roberts's manual labor. By having Scott's final scene in the film be one in which he joyfully proclaims that he "love[s] the smell of that sawdust," the filmmakers imply that this newfound vocation is a happy culmination of Scott's difficult past experiences. His voiceover explains, "I'm just—at work. This where I spend my time out; I spend my nights at home," confirming that Scott is learning the "habits of industry, thrift, and morality." In fact, as he is talking about how he "jump[s] straight to work in the morning," the camera follows his muscular body up a ladder on the side of the house on which he is working. As he ascends, his body is framed by the bright blue sky behind him. Lessin and Deal's choice to show this imagery of Scott's literal climb as he explains his current work reinforces their presentation of this scene as a metaphorical climbing and imparts the value they place on Scott's realization of the "dignity of labor." Although there is no inherent fault in Scott's choice of work, there is a class division inherent in this narrative, wherein it is implied that a man of Scott's socioeconomic background has reached his pinnacle in manual labor. Moreover, there is a problematic lapse into a recognizable narrative that reinforces racist beliefs and upholds the mistaken credo that individuals are capable of overcoming systemized discrimination by virtue of their own hard work.

Marlon B. Ross describes the central problem historically characterizing narratives that echo this philosophy of racial uplift:

> Although the Jim Crow regime is shown as clearly the one in error, the burden of change in the uplift narrative tends to be loaded on the shoulders of the racially stigmatized themselves. Washington, for instance, had urged the Black Belt residents to "cast down your buckets where you are," to prove themselves worthy of American freedom, prosperity, and inclusion by accumulating property through the performance of humble vocations of labor and enterprise. (Ross 2007:xxvii)

In *Trouble the Water*'s conclusion, the issues Ross describes here emerge in full force. Although the final scenes do level criticisms against the structural inequalities of pre- and post-Katrina New Orleans, the emphasis on Kim and Scott's individual success places the "burden of change" on the wrong shoulders. As Kevin Gaines has argued, "[a]lthough uplift ideology was by no means incompatible with social protest against racism, its orientation toward self-help implicitly faulted African Americans for their lowly status, echoing judgmental dominant characterizations" (1996:4). Especially given the propensity in post-Katrina news coverage and national discourses to blame the storm's victims (for failing to evacuate, for creating an environment hostile to rescuers, for not using recovery funds responsibly, etc.), a film that echoes this discourse of individual responsibility—even in seemingly positive ways, as *Trouble the Water* does—is dangerous in its proliferation of this dominant narrative, as well as remiss in its lost opportunities. Had the filmmakers resisted ending in this way, they would have a powerful example of a public adaptation of personal narrative that maintains distance, employing empathic unsettlement to deter the identification of viewers with its subjects. Instead, they ultimately deliver subjects who in their final appearances, if not their initial ones, are all too identifiable: as embodiments of a centuries-old ideology built on racism and classism.

Although the final scenes that depict Kim Roberts embracing her musical career are not as readily recognizable as the "humble vocations of labor," they do resonate with other aspects of the racial uplift narrative. Kim is shown smiling and nodding her head as the sound of her recently written song fills the room. The song's lyrics are about Katrina, and with a defiant tone ("we survivin' out here"), they comprise several critiques of the injustices she and her neighbors endured. As Kim is shown listening to her song, the camera zooms in on what appears to be new, sophisticated recording equipment, indicating increased financial success. In the next scene, the camera cuts to Kim driving a car. Viewers might remember that in the beginning of the film, Kim attributes her inability to evacuate to not owning a car, suggesting that this vehicle is new to her family. Thus, Kim and Scott are shown to be "accumulating property" as Washington's philosophy of racial uplift advised, putting them on track to "prove themselves worthy of American freedom, prosperity, and inclusion," ideals from which they were previously excluded. This conclusion offers a positive resolution to a struggle that becomes—unfortunately for Kim, Scott, and other survivors—no longer the audience's problem.

As Kim's music continues to play while she drives through the city, she is shown smiling and dancing in her seat until her car moves off-screen. Now the same city backdrop is crisscrossed by graphics of yellow caution tape, each one bearing statistics about the city's problems since the storm. This on-screen text informs viewers of the following points: "[B]illions of federal rebuilding dollars have not been disbursed," "rents in the city have doubled and so has the homeless population," "thousands of livable public housing units are being demolished," "most African-Americans have not returned while most white residents have," "the majority of the city's public schools are deemed academic failures," "Louisiana's incarceration rate is still the highest in the world," "and the rebuilt levees in New Orleans remain flawed and vulnerable." This litany, though accurate in its representation of problems facing the city, seems out of place given the rest of the film's conclusion. After the two preceding scenes, which emphasized the individual successes of Kim and Scott, this list is disconnected from these personal stories that viewers have been following. In fact, it reinforces the notion that Kim and Scott have survived and excelled despite the lack of structural changes. The next and final sequence of the film rounds out the concluding uplift narrative that makes this film dangerously pleasurable to viewers.

The film's final scenes show New Orleanians protesting conditions in the post-Katrina city, including a shortage of affordable housing and spiked rates of violent crime.[9] The camera pans across the crowd of people, including Kim Roberts. As horn players begin blaring an upbeat version of "Wade in the Water" and protesters parade toward City Hall, Kim's voiceover tells viewers that because of her family's displacement after Katrina and Rita, "we got to go see how other people was living. It opened up our eyes. I mean, it's like they preparing them for the future; here in New Orleans, it's like they preparing us for prison." During this voiceover and shortly after it, Kim is shown, first resolute and then smiling, holding a sign that reads, "Stop the violence." Despite the dismal truth of her realization, the context in which this quote is delivered gives it the air of a positive epiphany, a kernel of knowledge gained through hardship. Kim's voice and image imply that her experiences during Katrina have empowered her. This concluding scene captures an element of New Orleans second line parades, as practiced during traditional jazz funerals, in which participants celebrate in the face of loss.[10] But it does not show what happens next, as those who participate continue to mourn despite the joy they have expressed. Instead, as the film comes to an end, the brass band's horns grow louder, and the camera shifts from her to other faces, showing people laughing and dancing, landing on the final frame of an older black man, smiling and raising his hand triumphantly in time with the music.

Dominick LaCapra argues against this sort of resolution, and again in favor of empathic unsettlement, as follows:

At the very least, empathic unsettlement poses a barrier to closure in discourse and places in jeopardy harmonizing or spiritually uplifting accounts of extreme events from which we attempt to derive reassurance or a benefit (for example, unearned confidence about the ability of the human spirit to endure any adversity with dignity and nobility). (2001:41–42)

Although the film embraces this barrier to closure elsewhere, it indulges in harmony and spiritual uplift in its final scenes. LaCapra's choice of the word "unearned" is crucial to understanding the implications of *Trouble the Water*'s conclusion. The Robertses have earned the right to feel confident about their strength after being tested by Katrina, and they have discovered things about their abilities to survive that allow them to view themselves in newly admiring light. However, the audience has earned no such privilege, and having been removed from the suffering, they should not be allowed to reap its minimal, costly rewards.

Although perhaps well meaning, the filmmakers' indulgence in closure and a dominant narrative of uplift was not naïve. In response to an interview question about what attracted them to Kim and Scott as documentary subjects, Lessin and Deal explain the following:

> The Roberts and their friend Brian thoroughly defied the stereotypes we were seeing on TV at that time—the depictions of New Orleans' African American residents as either rampaging criminals or helpless victims ... [Kim and Scott] expressed a lot of hope and optimism, emotions that often seemed at odds with what was happening on the ground. (Lessin and Deal)

Lessin and Deal deserve credit for their awareness of the prevalent discourses characterizing Katrina survivors as either criminal or helpless and for their resistance of those categorizations. Like Josh Neufeld in the case of Denise, Lessin and Deal are conscientious about stereotypical representations of African American Katrina survivors. Also like Neufeld, though, they lose sight of how those identity categories are already being effectively negotiated by their subjects. The people on whom films like *Trouble the Water* focus, then, end up serving as "remarkable examples of good" to counter negative stereotypes (Hoeschmann and Low 2008:50). Kim and Scott are designated spokespeople for working-class, African American Katrina survivors, and they bear the burden of expressing "hope and optimism" to "thoroughly def[y] the stereotypes [Lessin and Deal] were seeing on TV at that time" (Lessin and Deal). What the filmmakers neglect is that storylines like these, whether in their positive or negative instantiations, have the same underlying logic: the burden (of being bad or good) is placed on the individual. Furthermore, presenting positive people and satisfying resolutions to their problems has the ability—and perhaps the intention—to "reassure the viewer" that the people portrayed "are not a threat to the existing order," the maintenance of which is ostensibly beneficial to the viewer (Hoeschmann and Low 2008:50). Like Booker T. Washington sought to do with his industrial education programs, these films placate presumably white, upwardly mobile onlookers with assurances that there is no danger to the structures that protect their privilege.

The conclusion to *Trouble the Water* has gotten the attention of other scholars, many of whom find it a problematic endorsement of neoliberalism. Geoffrey Whitehall and Cedric Johnson note that the film "follows a plot arch of trouble, tragedy, and redemption that most American movie-going audiences have come to expect," one that "resonates with the Christian Right, Obamanistas, and antiwelfare conservatives alike" (2011:61). Whitehall and Johnson cite the changes in Kim and Scott that are highlighted at the film's end, arguing that they are being made into embodiments of middle-class values and culture, and making the ironic observation that "ne'er-do-wells can assimilate to bourgeois culture if they are only given a chance" (62). Emphasizing how survivors, in the absence of government assistance, rescue themselves and each other in the film, Jane Elliot makes the case that *Trouble the Water* "is fundamentally about what it means to live in a neoliberal world in which such individual enterprise is offered as the only possible avenue of transformation or uplift" (2010:92). Elliot rightly identifies the discourse of individual responsibility that plagued Katrina survivors and was used as justification, in many cases, for their abandonment. She also offers insight into "the peculiar trap of neoliberal subjectivity, which can increase agency at the same time as it increases suffering" (91) and which, as a result, presents problems for those who believe themselves to be advocates of agency. Though for Elliot, her "point is not to impugn the documentary ethics of Lessin and Deal" (92), the fact remains that *Trouble the Water* ultimately celebrates the neoliberal model of "individual enterprise" as an "avenue of . . . uplift."

Some scholars note the potential benefits of embracing this model; Ruth Doughty describes *Trouble the Water*'s conclusion as follows:

> At heart, Kimberly Rivers Roberts' story is one of redemption. Prior to the storm, her and husband Scott Roberts were dealing drugs. However, the trials forced upon them by Katrina enabled them to start afresh, to be born again. This is witnessed at the conclusion of the narrative where Scott Roberts turns his back on gangster life in favour of becoming a carpenter, helping to rebuild his community. Kimberly is similarly seen creatively relaying her experiences through her rap lyrics. (2012:265)

Though Doughty finds this to be "a formulaic, generic blueprint practiced by Hollywood," she also notes its viability "as a marketing ploy" and its endurance as a familiar narrative (265). Janet Walker notes that the film "ends with an impression, however utopian, of integrated community" (2011:57). Bernie

Cook, following an otherwise astute analysis of the film's reflective qualities and its critique of Katrina's mainstream media coverage, seems to uncritically buy into the film's feel-good conclusion. Cook writes that "*Trouble the Water* argues that Katrina presented Roberts with the challenge she needs to reshape her life" (2015:211), a characterization that sounds too close to Barbara Bush's assessment of Katrina victims as better off after the storm. He also conveys the filmmakers' position that without their intervention, "Roberts would not have seen herself, or been able to construct herself as character" (212). The more precise issue is that without the narrative framework of closure and redemption imposed by Lessin and Deal, Kim Roberts would not have been a character that audiences could easily recognize, with a narrative they could comfortably consume.

Conclusion

The means by which documentary genres stake their claims to truth-telling are constantly evolving, and *Trouble the Water* exemplifies a trend towards self-generated content:

> Hopes of giving voice to the disempowered have ... long driven documentary film production more generally. Recent decades have seen this commitment take the form of increasingly participatory structures in which filmmakers give cameras to those who have traditionally been objects of others' representation and interpretation. (Hoeschmann and Low 2008:45–46)

Trouble the Water is unique as an example of these emerging "participatory structures" in that Kim Roberts handed Tia Lessin and Carl Deal a camera, instead of the other way around; as a result, the balance of power is productively disrupted from this film's inception. By including that disruption within the film, Lessin and Deal refuse to take their directorial authority back, and instead turn a considerable amount of control over to Kim as viewers watch.

Seeing the world through someone else's camera lens, though, does not equate to an unmediated experience of their life and worldview: the "assumption that access to the 'tools' ['means of information'] is automatically empowering ... glosses over the intricate politics of representation, of speaking and of listening, which inevitably shape all forms of cultural production and reception" (Hoeschmann and Low 2008:46). The inclusion of Kim Roberts's footage in *Trouble the Water* does not result in viewers seeing the traumatic events of Katrina as she saw them. As Jane Elliot puts it, "all of [Roberts's] self-affirmation does not give her the power to prevent her footage from being framed and reinterpreted once she has transacted with the filmmakers, nor does it give her the power to offer an on-screen interpretation of Lessin and Deal that would compete with or question their interpretation of her" (2010:95). However, by also incorporating some of the negotiations around Kim's footage within the film's finished product, Lessin and Deal take innovative strides in the production of personal narrative for public audiences. When they integrate Kim's commentary about her imagined audience, or scenes of Kim and Brian recording images unseen by viewers, they ensure that the "intricate politics of representation" are not obscured: neither for the sake of their own credibility nor for the benefit of viewers' comfort. The participatory structures employed in *Trouble the Water*, then, demonstrate how documentary genres might ethically represent traumatic experience via personal narrative. The film displays the potential of incorporating eyewitness accounts, along with the complexities and critiques inherent in producing those accounts for public audiences. However, it also exemplifies the limitations of imposing a recognizable storyline in the framing of such personal narratives.

Although *Trouble the Water*'s resolution makes the film appealing to audiences, thus ensuring broad distribution of these individual stories, it also reinforces a dangerous dominant narrative about individual effort as the antidote to systemic discrimination. Linda Selzer explains that historically, "the emphasis on self-help in uplift ideology, though admirable, also worked to shift responsibility for black people's condition away from corrupt social structures and toward supposed personal traits" (2009:681). *Trouble the Water* echoes this ideology by celebrating the post-Katrina return of Kim and Scott Roberts to their working-class, African American neighborhood, in which the socioeconomic conditions continue to place them at a disadvantage in terms of access to education, work, and social services.

Trouble the Water's conclusion reiterates the implicit promise of uplift ideology in its historical manifestations: "Through the accumulated efforts of exemplary *individual* behavior, eventually their white countrymen would see the good character, patriotic intentions, and indispensable economic contributions of the *collective* Negro race and reward them with full citizenship" (Ross 2007:xxvii, my emphasis). The film's emphasis on the individual successes and "good character" of the Roberts family becomes a plea for audiences to recognize this "exemplary individual behavior" and reward the collective to which the Robertses belong—poor, black, New Orleanians, especially from the Ninth Ward—with the benefits of citizenship denied to them during Katrina. Although Lessin and Deal effectively show the denial to Katrina survivors of those rights and privileges,[11] they also problematically position the audience to make a judgment about how and to whom those rights should be granted. Although viewers sympathize with the plight of the Robertses, their sympathy is too easily aligned with the "white countrymen" described by Ross above. Instead of bearing the "burden of change," the audience is evaluating whether or not the Robertses have earned the "reward [of] full citizenship."

The conclusion of *Trouble the Water*, given the context of post-Katrina New Orleans, perpetuates a victim-blaming discourse that prevented immediate aid and continues to impede recovery. In offering a harmonious resolution, the ending of the documentary undermines its early examples of LaCapra's "empathic unsettlement." One criticism that LaCapra might level, that the film's closure allows viewers to "derive reassurance or a benefit" (2001:41–42) from the traumatic experiences of the Robertses, would be relatively straightforward to address. Resisting closure would be as simple, for example, as concluding the film with a previous sequence, in which Kim gets approached by a police officer who instructs her to "turn the camera off" while she and her brother film a commemorative walk through their still deserted neighborhood on Katrina's first anniversary. Such a scene would imply that the recovery of these individuals and their communities is still ongoing, often at odds with powerful forces, the representatives of which continue to thwart residents' mobility, authority, and self-representation. Had the film ended in such a way, it would certainly have resisted a feel-good ending, though it may also have been less well received in professional and popular circuits.

The other criticism explicated here, however, begs a less obvious solution. The filmmakers attempt to showcase the agency of Katrina survivors, with seemingly positive rhetoric—similar to the "resilience" that characterizes official Katrina commemoration, as discussed in the following chapter. In celebrating these individuals, however, Lessin and Deal echo the ideologies of uplift and self-responsibility, and *Trouble the Water* keeps the "burden of change" placed on Katrina victims themselves. The filmmakers do attempt to shift this burden onto social structures and institutions in their examination of Katrina's response; the tourism industry, the military-industrial complex, and politicians at every level all receive their fair share of criticism in the film's evaluation of what went wrong post-Katrina. These criticisms allow viewers to feel righteously outraged, however, which creates an emotionally satisfying response, enabling inaction. The film's most uncomfortable and effective moments are those that make the audience complicit with the actions of these structures and institutions. Such a distribution of responsibility rarely extends to the audience, however, as the film proceeds, and Kim's footage is no longer central. Perhaps texts that adapt personal narratives of trauma for public audiences can expand LaCapra's notion of "empathic unsettlement" by extending the "burden of change" to be something that the audience must also bear.

CHAPTER FIVE

Not Written in Stone:
Tenth-Anniversary Commemorations of Katrina

Despite official and commercial attempts to contain and direct the memorialization of Hurricane Katrina, New Orleanians have resisted this homogenization in various ways. While visiting memorial sites and participating in tenth-anniversary events in 2015, I observed that the city's official anniversary slogan—"Katrina 10: Resilient New Orleans"—does not reflect the multiple vernacular modes of memory shared by ordinary New Orleanians. Just as with the publication of personal narratives, the public presentation of remembering Katrina tends to oversimplify and reify personal traumatic experiences. Official narratives of remembrance even echo the works of nonfiction that depict hurricane experiences, drawing on the same emphases on individual heroics and uplift. The attempts to solidify discourses like these in official memorialization show how critical it is to intervene in the circulation of such postdisaster publications, but they also provide an opportunity to observe how survivors are always already contesting these dominant narratives in their everyday lives.

Katrina's tenth anniversary, August 29, 2015, fell on a Saturday, and at least forty-five public commemorative events were scheduled throughout New Orleans, according to the local paper. Some of these events, such as an official wreath-laying ceremony at the Katrina Memorial, echoed the city's commemorative campaign of "Resilient New Orleans."[1] This campaign was widely visible via an official website, publicity efforts on mainstream and social media, and events throughout the month of August. In official venues, resilience was presented both as a product of local creativity and strength and as a response to global challenges for urban living.[2]

Overall, memorial events and spaces were characterized by conflicting modes of memory. A funeral home's attempt at coordinating handwritten memorial flags faltered, while a spontaneous handwritten sign appeared at an unsanctioned site. Tourists engaged in troubling renditions of vernacular practices at an official memorial. At a neighborhood ceremony, a government representative expressed her personal reservations about the city's public slogan. Even at the city's wreath-laying, one public official tapped into powerful personal memories by invoking sensory details of Katrina. At a second line in the Ninth Ward, participants openly resisted the message of "resilience," critiquing the officials who continue to disappoint them. And elsewhere, as in a commemorative workshop I organized during the anniversary week, New Orleanians revealed how other responsibilities, beyond that of remembrance, demand their attention. These multiple approaches to remembering Katrina belie the unified message of "resilience" and showcase instead the powerful nature of dynamic, critical memorialization—which, like dialogic moments in narrative representations of survivors, should be incorporated into public commemoration of disaster.

"In Memory of Daniel": Memorial Sites

On August 28, I visited the Katrina Memorial on Canal Street in New Orleans's Mid-City neighborhood. This memorial was built at the site of the Charity Hospital Cemetery, which had long been a burial place for many who died at the city's historic public hospital:[3]

> The cemetery had been used by Charity Hospital from at least 1843 to 1992 (George, 2002). It was originally known as Potter's Field (Salvaggio, 1992) and is the only completely subterranean cemetery in New Orleans ... [E]stimates [place] the number of burials at more than 100,000 because the cemetery was a primary burial location during the epidemic periods in New Orleans. (Heitger 2005:11–12)

This "potter's field" seemed a fitting place to Dr. Frank Minyard, the coroner of Orleans Parish at the time, when he was left with eighty-three unclaimed bodies of Hurricane Katrina victims. Minyard spearheaded efforts to build a memorial at the burial site, where a monument near the entry reads, "This memorial provides a final resting place for those whose bodies remain unidentified and unclaimed. May they have eternal peace."

The memorial itself, separated from busy Canal Street by an imposing black fence, consists of a paved walkway that spirals inward in the shape of a hurricane's formation.[4] This plan was designed by current coroner Dr. Jeffrey Rouse (Mustian 2015). At the "eye" stands a monument inscribed with a

Katrina Memorial fence on Canal Street. Photograph by author.

brief description of Katrina's deadly toll and Frank Minyard's creation of the memorial and a similar message as that found near the entrance: "The memorial received the remains of the unidentified and unclaimed victims and was dedicated to their memory on August 29, 2008. May they and other victims of Hurricane Katrina find eternal peace." Along the outer edges of the pathway stand six black granite tombs housing the individual caskets, which are "marked with serial numbers inside and out, should anyone ever seek to bring one of them home" (Stein 2015).

On August 28, the memorial was almost empty of visitors, with a couple of notable exceptions. Rows of white chairs under a nearby tent awaited the official ceremony that would take place the next day, and a woman in a bright orange "Katrina Survivor" t-shirt sat in one of the chairs under the tent's shade while I circled through the memorial. As I studied the markers near the entry, she approached and taped a sign, handwritten on blue paper, to a stone inscribed with names of organizations that funded the memorial. Her sign read as follows: "In Memory Of Daniel/who died because he could not/leave his 9 dogs behind. And for/the 50,000+ other pets that died <u>needlessly</u> in/ Katrina 8-29-05/Rest in Peace!" I spoke with the woman, asking her permission to photograph the sign, and our conversation quickly turned to Katrina. She told me that she had also refused to leave her pet behind (a still-living,

Stone marker with handwritten sign at Katrina Memorial on Canal Street. Photograph by author.

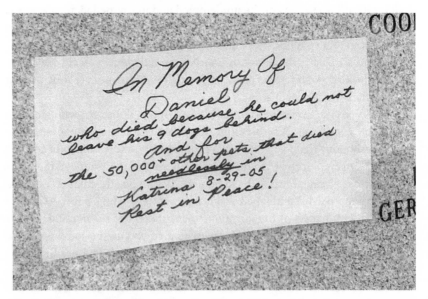

Handwritten sign at Katrina Memorial on Canal Street. Photograph by author.

now fifteen-year-old cat named Mr. Snuggles). She was not rescued until ten days after the storm, during which time she ran out of water and diabetes medication, causing her to permanently lose vision in her right eye. Rescuers eventually took her via lifeboat, then helicopter, then bus, to Tennessee. She told me that although she often visits the Katrina Memorial, she had not realized until that day that the remains were unidentified or unclaimed. Before that, she had always wondered why the names of officials (city government, donors, etc.) were inscribed at the memorial instead of the names of those who "gave the ultimate" (those who died). Although she did not tell me who Daniel was or what her relationship was to him, her commentary on the lack of victims' names suggested that she felt the need to "inscribe" one on her own—hence, the handwritten name, taped next to those etched in stone.

As I was preparing to leave the Katrina Memorial, a large Gray Line Tours bus pulled up outside the gate, and a tour group entered. The tour guide gave the group a brief explanation of how the memorial came about and then she turned on a somewhat muffled recording of "When the Saints Go Marching In." She encouraged the mostly white tourists to dance around the center of the memorial, in an attempt to re-create an aspect of the traditionally African American New Orleans jazz funeral. Few in the group participated, and those who did moved half-heartedly to the music. After less than ten minutes at the memorial, they reboarded the bus and took off for their next stop. New Orleans jazz funerals and the second lines that characterize them are powerful traditions, vernacular outlets for celebration and mourning and for voicing discontent, as a lively Ninth Ward second line held on August 29 clearly illustrated. But the touristic re-creation of this tradition among the quiet stones at the memorial was devoid of that meaning. As with the partial depiction of a second line in *Trouble the Water*, this rendition captured only gaiety (unconvincingly, at that) and no grief. The lack of knowledge about and investment in the tradition on the part of the tourists made its enactment ring false, making it almost a mockery of the place in which it was performed.

Lynnell Thomas describes moments such as this in pre-Katrina tourism, which included things like plantation tours and relied heavily on African American service-industry workers, as follows:

> Tourists were encouraged to think that they were experiencing and celebrating black culture by eating Creole cuisine, dancing to local music, participating in the traditional "second line" street parade, attending jazz funerals, and listening to anecdotes of quadroon balls and secret voodoo rites . . . New Orleans's tourism narrative, then, was part of the historically paradoxical construction of blackness

that acknowledges and celebrates black cultural contributions while simultaneously insisting on black social and cultural inferiority. (2014:7)

Thomas's study of post-Katrina tourism reveals this same tendency, despite
a moment of potential resistance to this tourism narrative immediately following the hurricane (150–51). She notes that even when post-Katrina tours
are "more inclusive of black spaces and stories," still, "the idea that all black
and white New Orleanians were unified and undifferentiated in their pre-
and post-Katrina struggles obscures a history of racial and class inequalities
and denies the persistent role of race and racism in post-Katrina policies"
(141). Bringing a busload of tourists to the site of burial and memorialization for unclaimed victims of the hurricane and engaging in the pretense of
a tradition that holds deep meaning for New Orleans's still struggling African American communities is a troubling attempt at celebration of black culture. As with the supposedly cohesive message of "resilience," such a practice
glosses over a diversity of experiences and masks the impact of racism both
before and after Katrina.

Tensions between official and unofficial memorials and between orchestrated and spontaneous commemoration marked other memorial spaces of
Katrina as well. Just half a mile away from the Katrina Memorial, though
it is separated from view or easy walking access by Interstate 10, is Metairie Cemetery and Lake Lawn Metairie Funeral Home. In stark opposition
to the pauper's field across the highway, this is the resting place of dozens of
local politicians and celebrities. One stretch of private mausoleums—housing
restaurateur icons Ruth Fertel (of Ruth's Chris Steak House) and Al Cope-
land (of Popeye's), among others—is referred to as "Millionaire's Row" (Lopez
2013). On August 28, 2015, the front of the cemetery was lined with rows of
small, white flags, planted in rows reminiscent of Arlington National Cemetery. Though the field of flags was highly visible from the nearby highway, as
was a large banner reading "Katrina Remembrance," the small signs inviting
participation were only legible to those who approached on foot. The signs
explained, "On the 10th anniversary of Hurricane Katrina, the staff of Lake
Lawn Metairie Funeral Home invites you to personalize a flag with your loved
one's name. To do so please come into the funeral home to obtain a Sharpie."
The white flag display was not unique to the tenth anniversary; in fact, the
funeral home did something similar the first year after Katrina and in years
following. In previous years, though, the flags already bore the handwritten names of Katrina's victims, rather than inviting people to write names
themselves (Oswald 2015). When I visited the flag display, it was late in the
afternoon on the day before the anniversary, and only a handful of flags had

Memorial flags at Metairie Cemetery. Photograph by author.

On the 10th anniversary of Hurricane Katrina, the staff of Lake Lawn Metairie Funeral Home invites you to personalize a flag with your loved one's name. To do so please come into the funeral home to obtain a Sharpie.

Sign near Lake Lawn Metairie Funeral Home. Photograph by author.

names written on them. In previous years there were 1,464 flags, representing the state's official death toll for Katrina; the number of flags appeared to be the same in 2015, making the seven decorated ones that I documented a barely visible exception in a blank sea of white.

Whereas the Katrina Memorial does not exactly invite spontaneous or informal interaction, the attempts of the funeral home to *dictate* such interaction proved to be even less inviting. Why was there a woman taping a handwritten sign to a stone memorial, when just down the street, an array of flags that were meant to be written on remained blank? Surely the settings are significant. Though both are formal—the memorial and the cemetery—the first has a history of being a place for common (even destitute) people, whereas the second is marked by privilege and wealth. The memorial is also more obviously accessible to passersby, with an entrance from the sidewalk near a busy intersection, whereas the entrance to the cemetery is designed for car traffic and is difficult to navigate. Furthermore, the sign at the cemetery instructs potential flag-writers to "come into the funeral home," which involves a walk across a parking lot to a building that most people would probably rather not enter for many reasons (the sadness associated with it, the potential awkwardness of encountering a funeral party, the inconvenience of having to find someone to borrow and return a pen). Perhaps most significantly, though, the flags present a fixed script, a unified display into which personal details might be entered. Similar to texts that collect individual stories into easily legible overarching narratives, the mass of flags offers the appearance of multiplicity while obscuring its true complexity. Placing a handwritten sign on a stone monument, on the other hand, makes visible both individual suffering and the contestation of the official narrative that represents it.

"The 'R' Word": Memorial Events

At the first tenth-anniversary ceremony I attended, early on the morning of August 29 in the Lakeview Neighborhood of New Orleans, the officially planned event drew city representatives and journalists, but few neighborhood participants. According to the *Times-Picayune*, the event was organized by the Lakeview Civic Improvement Association (LCIA) and was slated to begin at 7:30 a.m. with a wreath-laying, followed by a parade where "families [were] encouraged to wear red, white and blue outfits, and use these colors in decorating wagons, banners and signs" (Kleinschrodt 2015). Despite the presence of a fire truck, three members of the City Council, and five members of the press, the anticipated families with their decorated wagons were nowhere to be seen when the event began. Between ten and fifteen people from the neighborhood stood around and chatted for about half an hour, until Councilmember Susan Guidry made a few remarks.

As the small group of neighbors talked with one another, I spotted a former colleague from Delgado Community College who lives in Lakeview. She was surprised that there weren't more people present; she explained that it angers her when people do not want to talk about and remember Katrina. She and her husband, who lost and rebuilt their home, are not able to move past Katrina as the narrative of resilience suggests they ought to because they are in an ongoing legal battle with the levee board over their property. When people make the case that it is time to move on from the events of the hurricane, she thinks to herself, "How smug."

When I asked around further about the turnout for this Lakeview ceremony, one cameraman informed me that the organizers had participated in a race that morning; sure enough, a web search revealed that LCIA had a "Run to Recovery" scheduled for 8 a.m. that same day. Whether this conflicting schedule of commemorative events was intentional or not, it does speak to the larger trend in the city of multiple ways of remembering Katrina: there was no unified plan to remember the storm. Nonetheless, many public officials attempted to impose a unified message, in their insistence on the theme of resilience. When Susan Guidry spoke in Lakeview, she assured the small audience, "I'm not going to say the 'R' word this morning because I think my husband would leave." There were chuckles and groans in response; everyone present clearly knew she was referring to the city's official motto of resilience. Guidry's comment suggests the tension between official and unofficial commemoration: as a city representative, she is a spokesperson for that message, but as a neighbor and spouse, she recognized and respected people's aversion to it. Guidry wrapped up her remarks by apologizing that she had to leave to attend the wreath-laying ceremony on Canal Street and saying she hoped "LCIA and the gang" would soon be arriving with the Lakeview wreath.

I left at the same time as Guidry, also to attend the city's official wreath-laying at the Katrina Memorial on Canal. At this second ceremony, there was a much larger crowd, although politicians, other dignitaries, and members of the press still made up a large portion of the attendees. This event primarily espoused the city's official campaign of "Resilient New Orleans." During the ceremony, "resilience" was employed in the local sense, with officials applauding residents for exhibiting this quality and framing it not as a global strategy but rather as an innate characteristic of the region's inhabitants. Governor Bobby Jindal remarked that "the people of Louisiana and New Orleans are madly resilient and tenacious. They just cannot be held down" (Woodward 2015). Many others, such as Mayor Mitch Landrieu and Congresswoman Nancy Pelosi, gave speeches in the same vein. National news outlets picked up on the theme; the *Wall Street Journal* reported on the day's ceremonies by describing New Orleans as "[a] city known for its resilience" (McWhirter 2015).

One notable exception—to which the audience responded enthusiastically—was the speech delivered by Orleans Parish coroner Jeffrey Rouse.[5] Compared to polite, restrained clapping for other speakers, the crowd offered audible murmurs of agreement as Rouse recalled vivid details from the days following the hurricane. One reporter who also noted this wrote, "[T]he loudest applause from the crowd came for Jeffrey Rouse, the city's coroner. He asked people to remember 'the ungodly howl of the wind,' the rising waters, the heat and the 'dead floating face down'" (McWhirter 2015). Rouse also called on listeners to remember the smell of the city in those weeks following Katrina (a putrid blend of decay, death, mold, dust, chemicals, and more). Just as Susan Guidry's mention of "the 'r' word" drew groans from her audience, Rouse's departure from the ceremony's official tone drew outbursts signaling recognition and remembrance. In breaking from the frame of resilience and revisiting sensory details of memory, Rouse temporarily transcended the official script of overcoming and created a feeling of communal, spontaneous return to remembered experience.

The coroner's use of sensory details in his speech is interesting in the larger context of memory and memorialization. Beyond Proust's famous madeleine, many scholars of culture have approached the relationships between memory and the senses (for example Classen, Howes, and Synnott 1994; Seremetakis 1993; Sutton 2001). Most relevant to the present study, though, is Cristina Sánchez-Carretero's work on the 2004 Madrid train bombings (Sánchez-Carretero 2011). Sánchez-Carretero raises questions about the role of the senses in emotional engagements with public displays of mourning. In the case of Madrid, where spontaneous memorials of signs, candles, clothing, and other objects in Atocha train station commemorated lives lost in terrorist attacks, she explores how emotions can be expressed and internalized in embodied ways. She argues that when people left clothing at the communal sites of mourning in Madrid, they were "materializing emotions via [their] clothes, and depositing part of the emotional self at the memorials . . . linking body and memorial" (Sánchez-Carretero 2011:255).

Another interesting moment where bodies and memories interact, although one that Sánchez-Carretero only briefly mentions, is in the rationale provided by Atocha station's workers for why the makeshift memorial needed to be removed. Describing a letter published in a union newsletter, Sánchez-Carretero writes:

[W]orkers explain their trauma after the bombings, and say that the odor of the candles "entered into their lungs as an evil fluid." By having the grassroots memorials inside the station, they felt that they were working in a funeral chapel. The workers end their letter with: "We ask for the candles to be taken away from the main hall of the station, and a permanent memorial to be built nearby . . . We ask, in short, to be allowed to overcome tragedy." (251)

This example illustrates the powerful capabilities of smell not only to spark memory, but also to keep it alive, perhaps longer than survivors wish. Sensory experiences are, as Sánchez-Carretero shows, an important element of what makes unofficial, spontaneous commemoration powerful. When the Orleans Parish coroner asked people to remember the smell of post-Katrina New Orleans, then, he was invoking a vernacular tool of sensory memory. He was essentially doing the opposite of what the Madrid train station workers requested; rather than banishing sensory triggers of memory in favor of a permanent memorial, he was already in an official memorial space, inviting the smell back in. His audience's response indicated that he was effective in stirring up emotions and memory, at least more so than the other speakers who stuck to the script of resilience. People had an opportunity to revisit the embodied experiences of tragedy that they suffered, rather than being told to move on and overcome. The wreath-laying at the Katrina Memorial, when considered in its entirety, illustrates a partial incorporation of vernacular modes of memory into an official ceremony. The overall tone of that event, though, still echoed the official motto of resilience. The third and final memorial event that I participated in that day, however, was a clear departure from the city's prepackaged message.

Midmorning on August 29, I arrived at the levee near the intersection of Jourdan and North Galvez Streets in the Lower Ninth Ward. This was the site of the "10th Annual Katrina March and Second-line," which according to the local paper was sponsored by the New Orleans Katrina Commemoration Foundation, an organization initiated by local musicians and activists in response to exclusion from the city's official commemorations (Woodward 2015). The location was significant; rather than gathering at the area's official Katrina memorial, attendees gathered at the place where the Industrial Canal levee was breached, allowing water to suddenly and lethally flood the adjacent neighborhood.

The official memorial in the Lower Ninth Ward is a few blocks away from the levee breach, at the base of a bridge over the canal, in the wide median (referred to locally as "neutral ground") of North Claiborne Avenue. The "memorial complex" includes "a sculpture of a half-constructed house, a granite marker surrounded by two flagpoles," blue steel columns of increasing heights representing the rising waters, and on the partial house structure, a front porch with empty chairs surrounding it, representing "the celebrated stoop culture of historic New Orleans neighborhoods" as well as the absence of the neighborhood residents who would have sat in such chairs (Morris 2009:164). The Massachusetts-based architecture firm behind the memorial, Stull and Lee, explains the monument's origin and execution as follows:

> At the behest of New Orleans Lower Ninth Ward Neighborhood Council Inc. and City Council member Cynthia Ward Lewis, Stull and Lee designed and provided oversight for the construction of a monument to honor the victims of Hurricane Katrina and to *celebrate the indomitable spirit of the survivors determined to rebuild their community*. Designed and constructed in roughly three weeks, all of the professional services, materials and labor were donated. The monument was dedicated on the one year anniversary of the storm with the Governor and the Mayor in attendance in a ceremony covered by local and international press. ("Hurricane Katrina Memorial," my emphasis)

Although some critics find the memorial's celebratory message to be unclear (see Morris 2009, for example), the intended tone was one of resilience, the official rallying cry still heard nine years later. Perhaps the reluctance to embrace that message was partly why locals chose instead to assemble where the levee broke: they were physically revisiting the site of the breach and thereby calling attention to ongoing ruptures in their community.

Furthermore, the levee breach continues to be a site of contested memory regarding Katrina. Whereas official accounts attribute the levee failures to water overtopping levee walls and eroding the soil underneath them, unofficial narratives of survivors report that government officials exploded the levees, intentionally flooding working-class African American neighborhoods like the Ninth Ward to protect wealthier commercial and tourist areas such as the French Quarter. These narratives, though often dismissed by critics as outlandish, draw on the historical precedent of Louisiana's levees being dynamited with government support in 1927, protecting commercial interests at the expense of impoverished communities (see for example Barry 1997). They are also based on strongly held beliefs that a similar strategy was employed during Hurricane Betsy in 1965, as well as the empirical observations of Katrina survivors, such as those who describe hearing a loud boom shortly before the flood waters overwhelmed their homes (Lindahl 2012b). This contention that New Orleans elites were willing to sacrifice the lives of Ninth Ward residents was reflected not only implicitly in the choice to begin

Mayor Landrieu cartoon sign at event in Lower Ninth Ward. Photograph by author.

the second line at the levee, but also in explicit allegations such as those I heard shouted into a megaphone by one of the event's hosts: "They blew those levees on us!" Such resistance to official narratives characterized the entire Ninth Ward commemoration.

Upon my arrival at the Ninth Ward gathering, I immediately observed that this was better attended than either of the previous two ceremonies and that there was less emphasis on official organization and quiet solemnity. People spread across the grassy field below the levee, spilling into the streets. Vendors circulated, selling t-shirts and cold beer. Mardi Gras Indians greeted friends and posed for photographers. Once the ceremony began, with the hosts pouring a ritual libation, many people gathered near them at the top of the hill. However, music still played in the street below, and conversations continued among groups scattered across the field.

Even before the organizers began speaking and detailing the ways in which their communities were struggling and official recovery plans had failed them, it was clear that this event had a very different tone from the Katrina Memorial wreath-laying ceremony and that many of the politicians who had congratulated each other there on their progress were the subject of criticism here. Many people at the Ninth Ward ceremony were carrying signs (used as fans) decorated with a cartoon lampooning Mayor Mitch Landrieu. Landrieu is depicted as Pinocchio, with his telltale long nose bearing the text "recovery," indicating people's beliefs that Landrieu has been dishonest in rebuilding the city. The criticism is further specified by the images surrounding him in the cartoon: "luxury condos," "big box" stores, and the recently rebranded Mercedes Benz Superdome are presented as the mayor's priorities, while "affordable housing" and local architecture are destroyed, and "Mom & Pop" stores are "screwed." Other vernacular expressions of criticism were equally explicit; a t-shirt reading, "Where's my DAMN Road Home Money?" was an angry indictment of the federal program intended to help fund recovery efforts.[6]

With community activists such as rapper Mia X and Hip Hop Caucus president Reverend Lennox Yearwood leading the way, the ceremony included multifaith prayer offerings, music, and short speeches describing the community's challenges and enjoining those present to continue fighting for improvements. Mia X raised the issues of mental health and violence, commenting that "our children are hurting" (Woodward 2015). One speaker noted that the vision for recovery should be "our vision—not the vision of the mayor, not the vision of the gentrifiers." Community members were reminded that, regarding recovery and rebuilding plans, "either we are at the table or we are on the menu." The crowd responded affirmatively and enthusiastically to these messages, shouting, "Ashe" and rattling shakers.[7] As the ceremony built up to the beginning of the parade, organizers and attendees raised their fists in the air, chanted, "Power to the people," and made their way to the street following Social Aid and Pleasure Club leaders and Mardi Gras Indians in regalia. Dance groups and other musicians joined in, and the large crowd second-lined through the neighborhood, chanting, "Lower 9 still matters."

The range of traditional African and African American cultural practices drawn on in the Ninth Ward event, as well as the criticism of official Katrina recovery efforts, marks it as clearly different from, and in many ways opposed to, the wreath-laying ceremony at the Katrina Memorial. In contrast to the halfhearted tourist performance of a second line at that memorial as well, this second line performed by community members in the Ninth Ward was energetic and purposeful; similarly, in contrast to the meager turnout at the Lakeview Ceremony, the Ninth Ward event drew a huge crowd. At that Lakeview Ceremony, though, and even within the Katrina Memorial site and ceremony, similar threads of anger and resistance were expressed on an informal level: the handwritten sign "in memory of Daniel," my former colleague's anger at those who insist she move on from Katrina, Councilwoman Guidry's recognition that her family and neighbors were opposed to the "resilience" slogan, Coroner Rouse's departure from political speechifying to recall the sensory details of the post-Katrina landscape.

In part, such expressions are in response to the city's emphasis on resilience. This official motto suggests that recovery is going well and implies—especially in the way that it was deployed in the ceremony at the Katrina Memorial—that people are recovering well because of inherent qualities they possess, not because of assistance from government and other institutions. This is reminiscent of the theme of "uplift" in the conclusion of *Trouble the Water*. Chalking recovery up to "resilience" lets officials off the hook by implying that people ought to recover on their own—and if they do not, it is a personal failure, not a public one. Other scholars have called attention to problems with the concept of "resilience" broadly speaking; as Dorothy Noyes puts it, the discourse of resilience implies that "we are on our own—and the creek is gonna rise. . . . Its rise indexes the decline of institutional willingness to assume responsibility for the collective wellbeing" (2016:420). There are, of course, New Orleanians who do embrace the message of resilience and those who have exhibited this quality in the wake of the storm. However, the vernacular responses to Katrina's tenth anniversary are much more diverse than just this one slogan, and they express a wide range of emotional responses and modes of (not) memorializing the hurricane, whether that is anger at the inequality of recovery, or—as I encountered at Delgado Community College—attending to other pressing demands of ongoing everyday life.

"I'm Working That Day": The Antimemorial

On the day before Katrina's tenth anniversary, I visited Delgado Community College in Mid-City to conduct the Storytelling and Photography Workshop: Remembering Katrina. I had been an English instructor and writing tutor at Delgado from 2006 to 2008, and a few months in advance of the anniversary, I reached out to former colleagues for input on organizing a memorial event on campus. My goals were twofold: to create an alternative venue (apart from the official memorial discourse) where I could learn about how people were managing their memories and hear their opinions about recovery, and to offer some benefit to those who were willing to participate. Though my friends responded kindly with their ideas, some of them also expressed reluctance about participating directly because remembering the hurricane was too emotionally difficult; furthermore, they were already put off by the extensive coverage of the tenth anniversary, the resilience campaign, and citywide plans for commemoration.

I eventually connected with Melanie Deffendall, who directs the Irma Thomas Center for W.I.S.E. Women (Women in Search of Excellence) at

Delgado.[8] Inspired by the model of the SKRH project, I proposed an event where attendees would first participate in a training session, learning interview and photography skills, and then take photographs and interview each other about their experiences before, during, and after Katrina. Melanie agreed this would be a beneficial workshop for members of the Delgado community, and she generously offered logistical support, including space and publicity for the event. I also recruited the help of another friend, Matt Palumbo, a professional photographer who teaches math at Delgado. Matt conducted the photography training session, while I provided instruction in using recording equipment and conducting an oral history–type interview. Given the constraints of timing and structure, the interviews themselves were relatively short, and participants did not have the chance to develop the sort of ongoing relationships that were one of the valuable outcomes of SKRH. Most of the interviewers stuck closely to the questions that I suggested in the training session, further differentiating these interviews from the more open-ended "kitchen table" format of SKRH. However, the workshop was successful on many levels; namely, attendees were satisfied with the concrete skills they learned in the training sessions, and the interviews they conducted with each other revealed modes of memory that ran counter to the official tenth-anniversary campaign.

Twelve people attended the half-day workshop, and eight of those stayed the entire time and were able to conduct complete interviews.[9] The attendees were diverse in terms of background, age, and gender, ranging for example from a young Vietnamese woman who had just moved to New Orleans in 2015, to a thirty-two-year-old African American man who lives with his mother in the Seventh Ward, to a white man in his fifties from New Orleans who informed me as soon as he arrived that he did not appreciate when his professors tried to "indoctrinate" him with liberal views. Two of the attendees who conducted interviews had not lived in New Orleans at the time of Katrina: the woman who had recently arrived from Vietnam and a middle-aged man who had moved to New Orleans from Texas in 2012. This range of backgrounds presented a context for interviewing distinct from that of SKRH, where all the participants were hurricane survivors, and many times interviewers and interviewees were from the same neighborhood. However, all workshop participants belonged to the Delgado community, and this uniting feature was heightened by the setting of the event in the W.I.S.E. Center, which is well known and respected on campus, and by the presence of my coinstructor, Matt Palumbo, who had taught at least two of the attendees. These elements of community, along with the shared sense of being there to learn and practice photography and interview skills, created an environment where people felt reasonably comfortable talking with one another even when their backgrounds varied immensely.

Among the workshop participants who had lived in New Orleans during Katrina, most briefly mentioned the dramatic experiences and losses they had endured. However, there was not a single instance where such a mention resulted in an extended narrative describing harrowing experiences. In the recorded interviews, it is clear that interviewers are not interrupting their interlocutors or otherwise discouraging their continued talk. On the contrary, brief comments about difficult times during Katrina are generally followed by long pauses, an implicit invitation to continue if the speaker desires. In other cases, the interviewer will offer an encouraging remark, but in all these interviews, the conversation then turns to another topic. There are many possible explanations for this relative avoidance of extended hardship narratives. One, of course, would be the setting and the participants' relationships to one another. It is likely that in this short time, faced with the simultaneous task of learning to use recording equipment, participants were not comfortable enough to share their stories. As the extensive training in a context such as SKRH demonstrates, it requires substantial effort and time for survivors to break the mold of media-style interviews, of which they are rightfully distrustful, and engage in sustained conversation and storytelling (Lindahl 2012b). Furthermore, asking someone to reflect on commemoration while they are in the midst of it is asking for a challenging sort of removed perspective on one's own experience that people might find difficult. However, the "nonnarrative" moments in my Delgado workshop might also suggest that comments hinting at dramatic experience are unremarkable for the interview partners. The experiences to which they allude may, in the words of narrative scholars, not be "story-worthy" (Stahl 1989) or "reportable" (Labov 1982) in this particular context.

In perhaps the most startling example of a narrative *not* emerging, Raymond Chin interviews Carnisha Knox, who tells him, "I was here during the storm. Um, living on a bridge, people getting killed . . . that's about it." After a pause, Raymond offers, "Yes, I think that's—it was the . . . worst time in our lives." The two go on to discuss how those who stayed behind did not anticipate how bad the damage would be. Carnisha's references to living on a bridge and people being killed are not further explored. This avoidance may be due to the emotional toll of remembering those times, especially in this context, or it may be because the extended story that is implied is familiar to the listener and therefore does not merit further narration. This shared understanding is suggested when Carnisha interviews Raymond in turn, and the two conclude that if there is another hurricane like Katrina, they will move away and not return because, as Raymond puts it, "enough is enough"—to which Carnisha replies, "I know exactly where you are coming from." In another instance, Paige O'Brien interviews Terrell Gould. Terrell comments that he lived in several different places following Katrina, including Mississippi and Texas. Paige waits for further explanation and then follows up: "Okay. And what is something that you remember most about that time?" Terrell gives a brief general response about the "big impact" of the hurricane, ending with, "It was [an] experience that I won't forget." Paige continues, "Is that it?" to which Terrell replies, "Yeah." Here again, even with an explicit invitation to narrate his displacement, Terrell does not do so.

In the case of Duyen Thuy My Vu's interview of Jessica Faciane, the interviewer is a newcomer to the community and did not experience Katrina as a local. She remembers watching videos, as a young girl in Vietnam, of the roof blowing off the Superdome, flooding, and trees falling on houses. One of her reasons for attending the workshop, which she shared during the group's introductions, was to learn more about Hurricane Katrina from those who had lived through it. Contrary to most of the other interviewers, then, Duyen had minimal (and removed) personal experience with Katrina and an expressed desire to hear about others' personal experiences. Perhaps as a result, her interview of Jessica was the longest of all the interviews, and Jessica responds to questions with the most narrative detail out of any interviewee. Jessica recounts specific memories, such as "seeing one of my cousins, uh, break into the store so he could get food for my—for my family." She tells Duyen how it felt to see her family's home after the storm: "It was so weird seeing everything just so stripped away, like we saw the concrete and, like, no walls. They had to rebuild it . . . It's weird. Like right after the storm, we looked inside the house, and it had mold everywhere. Everything was just tossed over. We couldn't really salvage too much." Duyen actively positions herself as a curious outsider throughout the interview, asking, "Because I just move here, so I don't know really about that time, but I heard that some people they didn't move to another place. I don't know why, can—do you know why?" Rather than assuming her interviewer already knows the story of Katrina, as Carnisha and Terrell seem to do, Jessica offers a multifaceted response: "Um, they probably didn't want to. Like—like, some old people, they just, it's like 'this my home, I can't live nowhere else.' . . . Or they couldn't—they didn't have the financial stability to go somewhere else." This exception illustrates the rule that, generally, in this context, survivors did not recall their most dramatic experiences in detail, because those details were too painful to narrate in that context, or because those details were familiar to their listeners and therefore unnecessary to narrate, or perhaps due to some combination of both these factors.

In addition to the absence of extended narration, these interviews were marked by a lack of interest in participating in official commemorative events. The one interviewee who expresses something similar to the tone of the city's resilience campaign is G. Henry Renteria, who relocated to New Orleans from Houston seven years after Katrina. He remarks, "I think the city should celebrate the fact that they have come back from the terrible destruction . . . because it was pretty bad, brother. From what I have seen in the documentaries." This view is based not on memories of Katrina or continued personal struggles, but rather on G. Henry's impressions from published representations of suffering. Some workshop participants suggested specific traditions that would be appropriate to mark the tenth anniversary, such as eating a good meal or having a second line. Others emphasized that the tone of memorialization should be remembering, not celebrating. Paige explains that it would be appropriate to "remember the people we lost in the storm and, um, and maybe not too much celebrate, but hope that it doesn't happen again." Finally, both Duyen and Jessica exemplify that the demands of everyday life exist alongside the demands of memory. Duyen notes, regarding a citywide service initiative scheduled for August 29, "I really want to go there but, you know, I have to go to work." Similarly, Jessica explains her obligations as follows: "My job is actually hosting a lot of conventions for—for [the tenth anniversary]. A lot of organizations going to the Sheraton tonight [August 28], [to] celebrate the tenth [anniversary]." Duyen asks, "So . . . you gonna go to take part in some activities?" Jessica continues, "I'm working that day. Yeah, so I don't think I'll be celebrating, well, remembering. I'm just gonna be handing out food." In perhaps the ultimate display of the city's official events not resonating with ordinary New Orleanians, not only did Jessica not plan to participate in celebratory events, but she anticipated being too busy to remember Katrina because she would be serving visitors for the anniversary (presumably some from out of town, if they are attending a hotel convention) as part of her job.

Whether motivated by emotional avoidance, practical necessity, or deliberate resistance, these accounts demonstrate nonparticipation in official events that was echoed by others throughout the city. A *Times-Picayune* article from August 29 reported on New Orleanians who did not participate in commemorative events because it "was laundry day," they "had to work," the memories are of "the worst days" of their lives, or, as one survivor put it, "it's not like there's that much to remember, when it's all still here," indicating the ongoing struggle for citywide recovery (Grimm 2015). This is not to say the city's major commemorative events, including those beyond the wreath-laying ceremony described above, were not well attended. On the contrary, reports in the news and from city officials largely lauded both the mayor's community service initiative (Katrina 10: City-Wide Day of Service) and the celebrity-studded party at New Orleans's Smoothie King Center that followed (Katrina 10 Commemoration: The Power of Community), both of which drew thousands of people. An officially organized second line and block party also attracted large crowds and "achieve[d] full resonance" according to one reporter (MacCash 2015). However, away from these events where resilience was the unequivocal emphasis, many other New Orleanians opted for other ways to remember, or not remember, Katrina.

The living of everyday life, as opposed to participation in city-sponsored commemoration, ought not to be dismissed as mere ambivalence or apathy about Katrina's tenth anniversary. Or, more precisely, even if it is these things, it ought not to be seen as inconsequential. As de Certeau has articulated, the practices of everyday life, when viewed cumulatively and in relationship to dominant social and economic structures, are a form of creative resistance to those dominant orders (1984). Although analyses of news coverage of both the hurricane and its commemoration are important in their own right (see Eyerman 2015, for example), "the analysis of the images broadcast by television (representation) and of the time spent watching television (behavior) should be complemented by a study of what the cultural consumer 'makes' or 'does' during this time and with these images" (de Certeau 1984:xii). Thus, I asked New Orleanians participating in the Delgado workshop to discuss how they viewed news coverage of Katrina's anniversary. Their responses indicated their resistance, with G. Henry noting, "I don't keep up much with the news these days," or others noting that although the news made them aware of official anniversary celebrations, they had made other plans. Furthermore, considering how workers can manipulate their time based on "*modalities* of action" (de Certeau 1984:29), Jessica's assertion that she will have to participate in a memorial event for work but that she will not be "celebrating" or "remembering" indicates her ability to employ tactics of evasion: she cannot leave the official memorial event, but she can escape it (xiii).

Conclusion

Like Jessica and many others, I did not attend the Katrina 10 Commemoration at the Smoothie King Center. Even my own reasons are varied and not particularly easy to articulate. Perhaps most concretely, I was exhausted by the emotional toll of the workshop on the twenty-eighth and the three events

I had already attended on the twenty-ninth. I also felt the desire to be in a more intimate, familiar setting where we could choose whether or not to talk about our memories of 2005; I ended up spending the evening at a shrimp boil hosted by good friends. Leading up to the event, our friends exchanged emails about the best way to boil shrimp, and one of those emails displays some of the same conflicted and multiple modes of memory and commemoration discussed above:

> I've really been enjoying all the emails regarding the proper methodology
> for boiling one of the worlds simplest foods to cook ... I'm hoping to make it
> because I would love to see you all and eat some [shrimp]—but a certain some-
> one [ex-girlfriend] ... invited ... me to this 10yr anniversary event at smoothie
> center. I'm going to try to convince the certain someone that we should skip the
> commiserating smoothie king event, and attend an event that celebrates what's
> really important in life: Good friends and families getting together, nervously
> boiling shrimp, and getting 30+ yr old wasted.[10]

For this friend, revisiting memories of Katrina with a crowd would be too much "commiserating," and he preferred to spend the day forgetting (with the help of alcohol) and being in the company of loved ones.

The multiple memorial sites and celebrations described here do not suggest a single pattern of vernacular commemoration, but that is precisely the point. Official venues and events seek to present a unified approach to memory and a cohesive message of resilient recovery. They are consistent with a larger pattern, wherein "[t]raditions of public memorialisation—narratives, film versions of traumatic events, media reports, built memorials and commemorative events—typically cater to the 'softer' end of the emotional spectrum. . . . They foster admiration for bravery and endurance, and promote narratives of sacrificial heroism, so that the events in question acquire a redemptive aura" (Goodall and Lee 2015:8). Informal modes of memorialization, on the other hand, are spontaneous, diverse, and often critical of the notions that suffering has been redemptive, and recovery has been successful. Furthermore, "at a time when the rebuilding of New Orleans is uneven and incomplete, how we come to remember and forget the tragedy of Hurricane Katrina has far-reaching political and social implications, particularly for racial justice" (Thomas 2014:128). Just as published narratives of Katrina experiences seek to narrow down the multiplicity of personal experience narratives into easily digestible stories, and just as that process draws on harmful stereotypes, so too does official memorialization attempt to contain and concretize multiple approaches to memory and to present the stereotypical quality of resilience as the defining characteristic of the region, denying ongoing struggles or shifting the responsibility for those struggles onto the shoulders of survivors. Neither memory nor recovery is homogenous, and to present them as such is false and detrimental to continuing efforts to rebuild New Orleans.

CONCLUSION

Narratives of Katrina persist in American discourse. However, more than a decade after the event has receded from the constant media coverage of 2005, there are far fewer opportunities to reshape dominant patterns in how Katrina is understood. Stories that surface now tend to be interpreted in the context of earlier, widely distributed narratives, and acceptance of those narratives is apparent in rebuilding efforts. For example, rebuilding healthcare in the city has favored models that place the burden of change on the individual. Despite "the rate of mental health conditions like depressive disorders and post traumatic stress disorder among New Orleans residents" ranking "several times the national average" (Clarkson and Fielkow 2010:8.5), services related to "addiction recovery, developmental disability, and mental health" saw funding "reduced by several million dollars a few years after Katrina" (Clarkson and Fielkow 2010:8.9). In the same year, on the other hand, close to $10 million in federal and city funding were allocated for the increase of "healthy food choices," citing the problem that "New Orleans and Louisiana have particularly high rates of chronic diseases that are affected by food choice" (Clarkson and Fielkow 2010:8.10). The problems and solutions are framed in terms of individual choice, rather than availability of services. In an example of legal discourse, for prosecutors in the Danziger Bridge case to successfully indict NOPD officers for their murder of innocent civilians attempting to evacuate, they had to overcome the predominant belief that Katrina survivors were already criminals: police attempted to cover up the shootings with a widely accepted story that they were fired upon first.[1]

Katrina narratives still emerge in popular culture as well, including two incidents related to separate Super Bowls.[2] In 2013, former FEMA director Michael Brown shared a controversial comment on Twitter during a Super Bowl power failure at the New Orleans Superdome, and in advance of her performance at the 2016 Super Bowl halftime show, Beyoncé Knowles debuted her hit song "Formation," with a video featuring Katrina-related footage and images. Michael Brown wrote, "Someone just told me there was fighting going on in the NOLA Superdome. #shocked" (Gentilviso 2013). Brown's comment was interpreted as sarcastic derision, although nothing in the wording alone precludes his "shock" from being sincere concern. Because the dominant narrative of Katrina persists, though, his comment suggests that violent New Orleanians are again participating in self-destructive behavior as soon as the lights go out. Reports of violence among Katrina survivors in the Superdome, which were eventually shown to be inaccurate and exaggerated, were used as justification by government officials for their slow response, resulting in preventable death and suffering. Michael Brown was one such official who characterized rescue efforts as dangerous on this false basis. His sinister Twitter comment reinforces the erroneous and costly belief that New Orleanians are prone to violent, criminal behavior. Beyoncé's video struck quite a different tone, praised by many cultural commentators for its celebration of southern African American culture and defiance toward systems of oppression such as police violence. Part of what makes the video unique is the incorporation of footage that recalls home movies, featuring recontextualized snippets of New Orleans traditions and groups, such as bounce music, Mardi Gras Indians, and Black Cowboys, showing the creative persistence of these aspects of culture despite the devastation of Katrina (represented in the repetition of flood shots). As in *Trouble the Water*, this footage lends the power of personal experience and perspective to the work as a whole. Unlike in that documentary, though, there is no inclusion of the context in which those forms of cultural expression and resistance emerged or recognition of the ongoing challenges that they might face. It is too easy, then, given predominant understandings of Katrina that have solidified over time, for a video like this to be seen as one more abstracted monument to resilience.[3]

Together with the official and vernacular memorialization of Katrina discussed in the previous chapter, examples such as these illustrate the persistence and continued significance of Katrina narratives in the public realm. Not only do survivors continue to insist on the relevance of their ongoing suffering, but the stories that are in circulation about Katrina continue to wield discursive power. This study is an intervention in the deployment of that power and an illustration of how it might be redistributed. Survivors play a role in producing and circulating their personal narratives about disaster, and that role should be highlighted when accounts of disaster are published and memorialized.

The way in which survivors' stories are circulated matters to survivors themselves. In SKRH, Shawn half-jokingly anticipates that listeners may be in a position to help him rebuild his home. When presented with interpretations of his actions as heroic, Zeitoun continues to emphasize his ambiguity toward his experiences. In *A.D.*, Denise is concerned with how she may be seen as a stereotypical angry black woman. In *Trouble the Water,* Kim Roberts foresees the potential of her footage to captivate audiences, both those close to home (her future children) and those far from it ("some white folks"). On Katrina's tenth anniversary, some New Orleanians struggled to make their ongoing concerns heard, despite the city's official celebration of residents' resilience. These alone are sufficient reasons to critique existing methods of circulating survivors' stories. However, it is not only the survivors described here whose concerns are at stake. Because texts that adapt personal narratives present individuals as the face of larger groups, these narrators are made to stand in for broad, generalized categories. Audiences' reception of these narratives informs public perception of those categories, as well as public memory of the disasters that these stories describe. These texts also position their audiences in ways that prevent ethical engagement, empathic unsettlement, and productive response.

Ernst van Alphen writes the following, describing how stories from the Holocaust had virtually no impact on him when he heard them in his youth, because of the way that they positioned their listeners:

> First of all, war and Holocaust narratives were dull to me, almost dulled me, as a young child because they were told in such a way that I was not allowed to have my own response to them. My response in other words, was already culturally prescribed or narratively programmed ... The narration of this past had no ambiguities; moral positions were fixed. (1997:2)

Van Alphen's assessment of such narratives is strikingly similar to the issues that plague published stories about Katrina. In adapting those stories for wide circulation, the authors, producers, and publishers opt for fixity rather than ambiguity. Thus, the revelation of Zeitoun's domestic abuse comes as an utter shock, because his moral position as heroic has already been set in stone by Eggers's narrative. Josh Neufeld's graphic depictions of Katrina survivors are predetermined, or "narratively programmed," to be read as racial stereotypes in the cases of Denise and Darnell. Tia Lessin and Carl Deal, despite including disruptions of fixity at first, conclude by reprograming Kim and Scott Roberts's narrative to register with viewers as nonthreatening racial uplift. Official memorialization of Katrina unambiguously applauds resilience, allowing observers to feel good rather than face ongoing suffering. The effects of such positioning are not limited to the dullness or boredom that van Alphen describes.

As van Alphen goes on to explain, "[a]s the person who was being told these stories I was not interpellated, to use Althusser's term, as a human being

with moral responsibility" (1997:2). Similarly, audiences of public representations of Katrina are not called upon to feel morally responsible for the suffering in the narratives they consume. They are lulled into complacency by the
familiarity of the dominant narratives that absorb particularities of survivors'
experience, and they are permitted to indulge in feel-good empathy. These
are luxuries not permitted in the face-to-face narration of SKRH participants,
where survivors implicitly challenge dominant discourses and question the
effectiveness and reception of their stories even as they are being told. Narratives need not be shared in an interview setting to re-create this productive engagement, however; as A.D.'s web version and Trouble the Water's early
scenes both demonstrate, narrators' critique of their own processes of representation can be effectively incorporated into the texts that circulate those
representations.

   This is an important corrective to current means by which producers of
culture seek to create fair and ethical representations of real suffering. Vigi-
lance and conscientiousness are not sufficient to disrupt the power that
dominant narratives continue to accrue in contemporary American culture.
Eggers's insistence on the veracity of his accounts and their basis in Abdulrahman's actual experiences ultimately only serves to dull readers' capacity
for critique. Audiences accept the professed authenticity of this narrative as
confirmation that, because of their embrace of this male Muslim hero, they
are innocent in the perpetuation of stereotypical Western conceptions of
Muslim masculinity—the selfsame conceptions that are later summoned
to explain the domestic abuse charges against Zeitoun. Along similar lines,
despite Josh Neufeld's acute awareness of the history of stereotypical representations of African Americans in comics, he is unable to render Denise and
Darnell separately from that history. The white tourists second-lining at the
Katrina Memorial might be careful about using the correct music and moves,
but they are nonetheless doing the same old New Orleans dance, where African American culture is appropriated for the pleasure of white visitors and at
the expense of black communities.

   Incorporating survivors' negotiations within public narratives and memorialization of Katrina helps to counteract stereotypes and disrupt dominant
discourse. In SKRH, Patrice and Shawn contradict reductionist depictions of
survivors as either criminal or helpless. Their insistence on their responsibility is not apparent solely in the content of their respective interviews, but in
the interactive context of their storytelling. Studying this context reveals how
Shawn can draw his audience into the absence and discovery of knowledge
in Orleans Parish Prison, and how, after her initial confusion, Patrice emerges
as a highly competent narrator and actor. In the webcomic version of A.D.,

Denise corrects misreading of her emotional response to imminent danger, thereby complicating her depiction as a stereotypical angry black woman. In *Trouble the Water*, Kim challenges audiences to consider their own consumer interest in her narrative, as well as their participation in passive viewing of her plight and others like it in the national news coverage of Katrina. At a neighborhood commemoration of Katrina, locals satirized the politicians who, a few miles away, were congratulating each other for the progress of recovery. When these engagements are included in public texts and venues, they have the capacity to challenge official narratives, disrupt complacent empathy, and perhaps even shift the burden of change away from survivors.

Furthermore, the incorporation of survivors' negotiations into public representations can model the inclusion of their insight into the processes of rebuilding. As Carl Lindahl has argued in recent years, "survivors [may] help the institutional world—doctors, academics, funders—recognize ways in which the healing, teaching, and self-sustenance strategies of survivor communities may aid in disaster recovery" (Lindahl 2012a). My critique of the neoliberal narrative of resilience and self-help is in no way an indication that survivors are helpless, as should be clear from the stories documented here. Just as survivors are already narrating and remembering their experiences in ways that ought to be reflected in published accounts and official memorials, they are also already working to rebuild their lives and communities, and those efforts should be reflected and supported in official response and recovery plans. As the response to Katrina woefully illustrated, "authorities likely interfered with [the] ability of neighborhood residents and family groups to assist one another" because they were focused on the media narratives of criminality and helplessness rather than the effective strategies survivors were putting to use (Tierney, Bevc, and Kuligowski 2006:75). Instead, authorities can seek out "[t]he wisdom of lived, historical space—the kind of wisdom that knows what should be preserved and what should be transformed" (Gibson 2006:46–47). Recovery strategies that are generated within communities and those that draw on local knowledge are those that are most likely to succeed.[4] Moreover, social relationships and social memory are both integral to a community's recovery (Colten and Giancarlo 2011), and those who study responses to disaster in terms of "resilience" must recognize that resilience is socially negotiated and dynamic, rather than a preexisting condition or a one-size-fits-all model (Barrios 2014). However, until survivors are seen as creators and agents of change in their own stories, their contributions to recovery will continue to be ignored, opting for the continued reenactment of the dominant narrative of disaster response, where the collective wound is dressed from without, rather than healed from within.

In part, the shifts I argue for in terms of disaster representation are drawn from theoretical concepts of reflexivity. In the social sciences and humanities, reflexivity has gained popularity as a methodological approach. In general, researchers are more apt now to disclose and discuss the implications of inherently subjective analysis. Gillian Rose describes reflexivity as follows:[5]

> [R]eflexivity is an attempt to resist the universalizing claims of academic knowledge and to insist that academic knowledge, like all other knowledges, is situated and partial. Reflexivity is thus about the position of the critic, about the effects that position has on the knowledge that the critic produces, about the relation between the critic and the people or materials they deal with, and about the social effects of the critic's work. (2001:130)

But reflexivity in this sense is primarily an academic concept, and not one that has necessarily taken root in cultural productions, where the tendency continues to be either lack of concern with the ethics of representation, or, more along the lines of Dave Eggers's approach, a meticulously documented claim to accurate representation. I am not arguing here for the adaptation of explicit reflexivity in all artistic or cultural expressions; such a claim would obviously be futile and contrary to the goals and methods of plenty of artists. However, where artistic production mimics the methods and claims to legitimacy of academic research, I believe this critique and argument are warranted. More specifically, if texts purport to emerge from extensive interviews with real people, mirroring ethnographic research and methods, then those texts ought to also include the turn that ethnography has taken to the reflexive, the reciprocal, the dialogic.

Elaine Lawless has famously written about the necessity for this turn in the field of folklore studies. She advocates for "the critical importance of a new ethnographic approach that will not only direct our methodology, but also inform our interpretations and dictate the presentations of our conclusions" (Lawless 1992:313). She continues, "[I]f we insist upon interpreting other people's interpretations, at the very least, we are obligated to allow them space to respond" (313). Lawless illustrates this approach, which she labels reciprocal ethnography, by publishing an article that includes a response to her findings by Sister Anna Walters, a participant in her study on Pentecostal women. In short, after publishing and sharing the final product of her research, Lawless was surprised to hear from Sister Anna that she objected to and disagreed with some of Lawless's interpretations. Therefore, in a subsequent article, Lawless includes both her own interpretations and Sister Anna's commentary on those interpretations, and Lawless argues for the adoption of this dialogic practice, at earlier stages in research, by others in the field. As she puts it, not only does "[t]he final phase of the hermeneutic circle . . . [demand] that we subject our interpretations to the interpretations of our subjects" (Lawless 1992:313), but also those processes of interpretation must make their way to audiences. My argument is like Lawless's in that I also argue for the inclusion of this dialogue in the final product. I advocate for this shift in nonacademic genres, though, and I advocate not only for dialogue about content, but also for explicit engagement regarding the processes of production, circulation, and reception of texts. Whereas readers of Lawless's article see Sister Anna's objections to certain descriptions of her lifestyle, they do not see any critique by Sister Anna of who might read these descriptions, how, and to what ends. Thus, my claims, in comparison to Lawless's, are more focused on process than product.[6]

My proposition, then, is for a dialogic approach to processes of narrative production, circulation, and reception in contexts of public disaster. As observers and critics, we can bring attention to the dialogue that already exists by investigating negotiations regarding narrative distribution and consumption. These may take the shape of appeals to credibility, anticipated responses to narratives, or invitations or reproaches directed at particular audiences. For producers of personal disaster narratives, this means that texts should incorporate dialogue, even when contentious, with the narrators whose stories they publish. Rather than attempting to ward off stereotypes through ineffective avoidance, texts can better interrupt dominant narratives by making evident the means by which survivors themselves engage them. In taking up personal narratives and circulating them for public consumption, distributors ought to be more aware of their mediating role. It is impossible, as many seem to presume, for them to erase their influence on the stories they share. They can, however, recognize that in their recontextualization of a narrator's performance, they have disrupted that narrator's relationship of accountability with a particular audience. Instead of trying to mimic that relationship in a new context by creating the illusion of direct communication, they can assume their own responsibility—in a process that is more ethical and ultimately more effective in terms of redistribution of social power—by including in their publications the processes by which recontextualization occurs.

Because I am arguing for a more reflexive and dialogic approach to the public circulation of personal narratives, those qualities inform my own production of this work.[7] First, in my analysis of texts, I do not limit the scope of my study to the text itself; rather, I examine the interactive contexts of these narratives' production, circulation, and reception. As a result, my thoughts as a reader and viewer are constantly in dialogue with the responses of other audiences, and I incorporate these other interpretations throughout my study.

In my chapter on SKRH, I include the questions and responses of interviewers; my discussion of *Zeitoun* includes the responses of reviewers to that text; the chapter on *A.D.* integrates webcomic readers' online comments; and my study of *Trouble the Water* describes the film's critical reception. To further expand and challenge my own experiences of reception with respect to these texts, I have incorporated some of them into my teaching of undergraduate courses. Observing my students' responses to *Trouble the Water* and *A.D.* helped to balance my own perspective as someone very familiar with the historical event of the hurricane. My students, by virtue of their age (generally between eighteen and twenty-two) and their geographic location (primarily American Midwest at the time), were less likely to approach the texts with extensive prior knowledge about Katrina and New Orleans.

Furthermore, I have sought out dialogue with survivors of Katrina from New Orleans, most notably in the fieldwork described in chapter 5. Prior to that, though, given my personal experience as an evacuee, I have had continuous access to friends, family, and acquaintances with whom I discuss my thoughts and test my conclusions, especially regarding popular conceptions or misconceptions about Katrina and concerning the reception of the texts I examine here. It was from those conversations, as well as from my volunteer work with elementary school children and my teaching of local college students, that I first gathered that New Orleanians were frustrated with the difficulties they faced in trying to articulate their experiences. These frustrations were primarily attributed to misunderstandings on the part of listeners, rather than an inability to talk about what they had been through. This pattern contradicts a prevalent general understanding of trauma, which has it that obstacles to narration of traumatic experience essentially arise from within: because of the way in which traumatic events are disruptive to their survivors, those individuals struggle in making sense of them, narratively or otherwise. But the conversations I was having led me to reexamine this basic model and ask what external, or social, conditions encouraged or restricted survivors' narration. As a result, I arrived at this study of interactional contexts of narrative production and the public circulation and reception of personal narratives.

As my research progressed, I shared and adjusted my interpretations in public venues, especially in dialogue with the survivor-narrators of SKRH, with whom this book begins. Despite the difficulties of locating and contacting interviewees, who as evacuees were transient, I hope and aim to continue conversations about the findings presented here. In October 2012, I copresented on a conference panel in New Orleans with participants from SKRH. I described the conclusions I was reaching and invited discussion in response.

I found that one claim that resonated particularly with the survivors who were present was their continued misrepresentation in public discourse, especially the news media. They agreed emphatically that part of the motivation to continue telling their stories was the belief that their experiences had not been accurately or justly translated beyond their own communities. They also expressed a desire to share their strengths, as well as their continued struggle, with others who endured disastrous events. Survivors of the 2011 Japanese earthquake and tsunami were also part of this panel, and Katrina survivors offered them commiseration and encouragement.

As part of that same conference meeting, our group of survivors and scholars of disaster took a tour of New Orleans's most devastated neighborhoods. Ironically, at a time when city officials were finally responding to residents' demands to shut down the commercial "Katrina tours" that were viewed as a voyeuristic obstacle to resuming normal life, these survivors were enthusiastic about leading us on a tour of their neighborhoods. Because the guides were themselves survivors, pointing out their own flooded homes, this tour was premised on a different sort of relationship than those that bussed in tourists to drive by and photograph a destroyed house, whose residents they knew nothing about.[8] This is not to say that our trip was free of any of the problems inherent in disaster tourism, but rather to point out that survivors welcomed the opportunity to narrate on their own terms and engage with the story that was being told to audiences of their suffering.

Midway through that tour, our group stood outside the home of local musician Al "Carnival Time" Johnson (nicknamed for his 1960 hit song). As a survivor who evacuated to Houston, Johnson had contributed an interview to SKRH. I transcribed that interview, the majority of which Johnson spent lamenting the legal battles wherein he spent nearly forty years trying to regain the rights to the music he created as a young man.[9] In the interview, Johnson did not say much about his experiences during Katrina, nor has he been a public spokesperson for the city's troubles, as have some other local musicians. However, on a sunny Wednesday afternoon in October, on the sidewalk outside his home, Johnson was ready and willing to discuss his ordeal. This example demonstrates for me the significance of context for narrative production. What was it about that setting that enabled Johnson's narrative to emerge? Was it the physical location, the geographical proximity to the scene of his survival? Was it the timing, the temporal distance from the remembered events? Did it have to do with the audience, the interested visitors, including several survivors of the Japanese disaster from across the globe? Was it the stories that others were telling as we stood there, creating a discursive environment in which the language of his experience belonged?

These types of questions interest me, and they have driven my analysis of the full range of texts and practices included here. As a final reflection, however, I will add that in that moment, my own narrative about Katrina did not emerge. Those conditions that produced Al Johnson's story were not the same conditions that would produce my story, and in the spirit of reflexivity, I consider why that might be. The stories being told in that setting sufficiently distanced me—successfully produced empathic unsettlement—so that I did not identify with Johnson's narrative and feel compelled to share my own. Johnson's specificity, his grounding in the particulars of the house—whose weathered sideboards were visible behind him as he spoke—did not invite a generalized reading of his experiences. His appeal to the Japanese survivors who were present was about the need to carry on despite being surrounded by signs of ongoing struggle; given my own relocation outside of New Orleans, this was not an appeal that applied to me. Thus, the narrative strategies he employed created a context of production that positioned me as an outside observer: any connection I might feel was rendered irrelevant by the framing of his story. I am aware that this is not a feel-good ending moment, a beautiful note of reconciliation, inclusion, and recovery. However, I find that particularly fitting, because the distance and discomfort in that narrative interaction is indicative of my questions, my methods, and my conclusions.

Personal narratives of disaster *should* make us uncomfortable, because disaster should make us uncomfortable as we recognize our limitations with respect to it. Disasters do not turn us into monsters, and they might well bring out admirable traits within us.[10] But they also do not make us into one-dimensional heroes or pillars of resilience. Rather, they provide an intensified and threatening context for all those complicated qualities that make us human and tie us to one another. When we represent and remember disasters, it is important not to render those complexities and connections invisible. As personal stories become public ones, we need to work to preserve the interactive contexts from which they derive meaning. These personal narratives are already public in many senses of the word: the relationships they describe, the audiences they envision, the influences they reflect. Our job is to do justice to those dynamic social elements, rather than fall for the façade of the perfectly representative personal story. If we do not, we risk allowing survivors to be used as tools for their own continued suffering, rather than empowering them in their work toward recovery.

NOTES

Introduction

1. See https://www.fema.gov/news-release/2006/08/22/numbers-one-year-later. More than 1 million people were displaced from the Gulf Coast region. Although reports differ, most place the death toll in Louisiana between one thousand and fifteen hundred. In New Orleans, which is my focus here, 80 percent of the city was flooded by the compromised levee system, and residents were stranded in terrible conditions for days, awaiting rescue.

2. This archive of interviews, conducted with hurricane survivors displaced to Texas, is described in more detail in chapter 1.

3. Carl Lindahl, cofounder of SKRH, has made this argument repeatedly, and this belief was the impetus for his spearheading the formation of the International Commission on Survivor-Centered Disaster Recovery (see http://www.survivorcentered.com/).

4. See for example Dahmen and Miller (2012), who write that in both 2005 and 2010, the focus of Katrina anniversary coverage was on "survivor stories" or "*people* who had survived the storm" (10). Significant work related to these issues has been done in the areas of testimony and witnessing (Gilmore 2001; Oliver 2001; Beverley 2004; Yaeger 2006; Assmann 2006); memory and narration of genocide (Felman and Laub 1992; Rothberg 2009); and use of personal narratives in human rights contexts (Schaffer and Smith 2004; Hesford 2011). Although these are fascinating and relevant areas of research, my focus is on personal narratives of disaster that are adapted and published for a wide audience.

5. See for example Garfield 2007; Negra 2010; Kverndokk 2014; Cook 2015; and Eyerman 2015. Kai Erikson and Lori Peek have compiled a very thorough bibliography, including sources on media coverage of Katrina and a wide range of other "reference information for reports, journal articles, book chapters, and books that explore the human effects of Hurricane Katrina" (Erikson and Peek 2011:2).

6. Suzanne Seriff also curated an exhibit titled *The Arts of Survival: Folk Expression in the Face of Natural Disaster* at the Museum of International Folk Art in 2011–12 that included work by a New Orleans folk artist among others (http://www.internationalfolkart.org/exhibition/1056/the-arts-of-survival-folk-expression-in-the-face-of-natural-disaster).

7. Amy Shuman identifies a similar pattern characterizing hearings for asylum seekers (2008).

8. Tonkin proposes that "[t]he missing term in Halbwachs' account is socialisation, which I would define as the ways and means by which we internalise the external world" (1992:105).

9. Beiner also cites James Fentress and Chris Wickham's use of the term "social memory" and points out the added benefits of that term's distance, as opposed to Halbwachs's "collective memory," from Carl Jung's notion of a collective unconscious (2007:27).

10. In Niall Ó Ciosáin's study on folklore and memory of famine in Ireland, he writes, "As the memory of the Famine was transmitted, it was probably those elements of local memory that corresponded most closely to popular memory that were most 'tellable,' that survive in the narrative repertoire of the informants" (2004:226).

11. For scholarly reviews regarding these terms and approaches, see, for example, Phillips (2004), especially Edward Casey's contribution to the volume, and Olick and Robbins (1998). On public memorialization and museums, see Dickinson, Blair, and Ott (2010) and Haskins (2015).

12. See for example Bal, Crewe, and Spitzer (1999); Kaplan (2005).

13. Dominant theories of trauma in the past rested on the foundations of individual injury, as in "railway spine," and individual treatment, as in psychoanalysis. PTSD, despite its diagnostic origins in soldiers' shared experience of war, is still tied to an understanding of trauma as an individual affliction. For a review of this history, see Young (1995) and Caplan (1995).

14. Fassin and Rechtman point out that "recognition of trauma, and hence the differentiation between victims, is largely determined by two elements: the extent to which politicians, aid workers, and mental health specialists are able to identify with the victims, in counterpoint to the distance engendered by the otherness of the victims. . . . [T]rauma, often unbeknownst to those who promote it, reinvents 'good' and 'bad' victims, or at least a ranking of legitimacy among victims" (2009: 282).

15. Erikson also argues that "trauma" should be understood in terms of effects rather than causes, which would allow that a disaster's "victims" are those who suffer, not necessarily those who are designated by external criteria such as proximity to the event. This differs significantly from the clinical definition of PTSD, as Allan Young points out (1995:7). Instead, Erikson argues that "it is *how people react to them* rather than *what they are* that give events whatever traumatic quality they can be said to have" (1994:229, emphasis in original).

16. See also de Lauretis (1984); Sawin (2004).

17. My methods are influenced by Bauman and others who study the performance of a text in the hopes of "freeing it from the apparent fixity it assumes when abstracted from performance and placed on the written page" (1975:303; see also Ben-Amos 1971; Dundes 1980; Bauman 1986; Cortazzi 2001).

18. This sociolinguistic approach of critical discourse analysis is explained by Norman Fairclough as a "'three-dimensional' framework where the aim is to map three separate forms of analysis onto one another: analysis of text, analysis of processes of text production, distribution, and consumption, and analysis of context (1995:211); see also Schiffrin, Tannen, and Hamilton (2008).

Chapter One: "Establish Some Kind of Control": Survivor Interviews

1. For discussion of additional documentation efforts related to Hurricane Katrina, and of issues pertaining to oral history projects in the wake of disasters, see Stein and Preuss, "Oral History, Folklore, and Katrina" (2008).

2. I use pseudonyms for the interviewees and interviewers throughout to protect the interviewees' identities, according to their wishes. Many other contributors to the SKRH archive, however, did wish their names to be associated with their stories. Some of those remarkable stories and people can be found online (http://survivingkatrinaandrita.dgs-sites .com/index.php), and others have been published in *Second Line Rescue* (2013) and in *Callaloo* 29.4 (2006).

3. Carl Lindahl and Pat Jasper hired me to help transcribe and catalogue SKRH interviews between 2009 and 2011, which provided me access to these and more than four hundred other narratives.

4. This is Alan Dundes's often-cited terminology from *Interpreting Folklore* (1980).

5. Hill and Zepeda are citing Chafe's (1980) use of "story world" and "interactional world."

6. Hill and Zepeda cite Tannen (1998).

7. Jane Elliot notes a related pattern in Spike Lee's *When the Levees Broke*; she argues, "Through the emphasis on interviewees as narrators, agency becomes associated with an act of *describing* an experience of suffering" (2010:106).

8. Patrice references gathering information from the news previously in the interview.

9. Multiple psychological studies have investigated the role of religion in people's responses to and recovery from disaster broadly, and from Hurricane Katrina specifically. For example, S. W. Cook and colleagues conclude in their post-Katrina study that "religious comfort (i.e., maintaining a positive relationship with God) was generally associated with positive adjustment and even buffered the impact of resource loss" (2013:360). Similarly, another study that spanned Katrina found that "in the face of a devastating event, religiousness provides a sense of optimism and purpose that might have helped the survivors maintain their psychological health" (Chan, Rhodes, and Pérez 2012:177). Such studies suggest that Patrice's concerns may reflect broader patterns in disaster-affected communities. It is also interesting to note, however, the attention such studies pay to intangible rather than material resources; as Dorothy Noyes notes, "comparable studies with similar findings seem never to have been conducted of, say, investment bankers after the subprime mortgage crisis of 2008" (2016:423).

10. Metairie is within Jefferson Parish, and New Orleans is in Orleans Parish. Jefferson Parish officials, allegedly with the support of then-sheriff Harry Lee, notoriously used force to prevent many evacuees from crossing parish lines.

11. In his fascinating example, a scene from *Full Metal Jacket* (Stanley Kubrick's 1987 film) informs his interpretation of a vintage postcard depicting hunters with their prey (Mechling 2004).

12. For more on the alleged explosion of New Orleans levees, see Hirsch and Levert (2009) and Kelman (2009). For a relevant and insightful discussion of the intentional flooding of the rural African American town of Pinhook, Missouri, see Lawrence (2015). Lawrence writes, "There was no formula in which the people of Pinhook could register significant enough value to forestall the operation of the floodway . . . Our contention, though, is not that Pinhook was unfairly undervalued in the consideration of whether to breach the levee, but that because of Pinhook's status as a black rural town, its very existence was overlooked" (230).

13. See, for example, the work of the International Commission on Survivor-Centered Disaster Recovery (http://www.survivorcentered.com/).

Chapter Two: From "Angel of Mercy" to
"Fallen Folk Hero": Zeitoun's Story Travels

1. In fact, I noted on a recent visit to my local public library that these books were two in a small handful making up the Louisiana section of the American history bookshelf.

2. See Goffman, *The Presentation of Self in Everyday Life* (1959). It is not necessary, or perhaps even possible, to know Zeitoun's motivations for presenting himself in a particular way: for example, Goffman writes, "Sometimes the individual will act in a thoroughly calculating manner, expressing himself in a given way solely in order to give the kind of impression to others that is likely to evoke from them a specific response he is concerned to obtain. Sometimes the individual will be calculating in his activity but be relatively unaware that this is the case. Sometimes he will intentionally and consciously express himself in a particular way, but chiefly because the tradition of his group or social status require this kind of expression and not because of any particular response" (6).

3. Dan Bright was arrested on misdemeanor charges during Hurricane Katrina, then endured a long ordeal like Zeitoun's, in part because prison officials either were unaware of or willfully ignored his exoneration for his prior charges. His release was ultimately secured by Billy Sothern's legal office.

4. This language appears in multiple places, including in Vollen and Ying (2006) and on the website http://voiceofwitness.org/.

5. See Schaffer and Smith (2004) for examples and an analysis of these patterns.

6. The appendices comprise information like maps, demographics, National Weather Service warnings, and government agency reports and meeting transcripts.

7. Although a second edition of this book was published in 2008, after charges were brought against New Orleans Police officers, this language remained the same.

8. Gillian Whitlock (2007) defines paratext, following Gerard Genette, as "the liminal features that surround and cover the text" (14).

9. See Gaudet (2013) for an insightful discussion of Lieutenant General Russel Honoré, commander of Joint Task Force Katrina, as a folk hero in the wake of Katrina.

Chapter Three: Katrina Stories Get Graphic in
A.D.: New Orleans after the Deluge

1. *Smith Magazine*'s editor, Larry Smith, sought out Neufeld after reading "Katrina Came Calling," the author's "self-published zine about [his] time volunteering with the Red Cross in the Gulf Coast after the hurricane" (Neufeld 2009:191). Smith thought Neufeld would be perfect to document real life experiences of the hurricane, although in *A.D.*, Neufeld leaves behind his own volunteering story and focuses instead on survivors.

2. These are the names used in the published book. In the webcomic version of *A.D.*, Kwame (real name) is Kevin, Abbas is Hamid (real name), and Darnell is Mansell (real name).

3. Coby's larger point is about how the hyperlink that Neufeld provides on the webcomic version of this panel no longer functions; he argues that this creates frustration for webcomic readers that parallels the confusion of those who did not have access to this

type of information during Katrina, enabling readers to better understand that experience (2015:119–20).

4. See, for example, http://www.nbcnews.com/id/10074295/ns/us_news-katrina_the_long_road_back/t/months-later-victim-katrina-laid-rest/#.V4lKqpMrKb8.

5. Anthony Dyer Hoefer also writes about this exchange between Denise and Dean Haspiel. It is interesting to note that scholarly discussion of such apparently striking commentary is also precluded in the print version of *A.D.*

6. Darnell is also absent from the report, an omission on which Neufeld does not comment (http://fusion.net/story/190071/where-are-they-now-revisiting-4-hurricane-katrina-survivors-10-years-later/).

Chapter Four: "They Probably Got Us All on the News": Unsettled Filming in *Trouble the Water*

1. According to boxofficemojo.com, a subsidiary of the Internet Movie Database (IMDB), *Trouble the Water* grossed $522,766 worldwide in its nine-month theater run, ranking it 187th of more than 1,000 listed documentaries. The film was also nominated for an Academy Award for Best Documentary Feature and was the winner of the Grand Jury Prize for Best Documentary at the 2008 Sundance Film Festival.

2. This discourse covers a wide spectrum, from remarks like former Speaker of the House Dennis Hastert's comment that "a lot of that place could be bulldozed" to the Bring New Orleans Back Commission's proposal to reduce the city's "footprint" (see http://www.nbcnews.com/id/9164727/ns/us_news-katrina_the_long_road_back/t/hastert-questions-proposed-efforts-rebuild/ and http://www.bgr.org/news/archives/officials-tiptoe-around-footprint-issue/, respectively).

3. This remark also proved to be prescient: Kim and Scott's first child was born at the Sundance festival at which *Trouble the Water* premiered (see http://www.rollingstone.com/movies/videos/sundance-a-star-is-born-20080125).

4. See http://blog.nola.com/mikescott/2009/03/9th_ward_couple_relishes_road.html.

5. Maurice Stevens (2006) and Rebecca Wanzo (2009) both describe media coverage of Katrina victims as "illegible" to viewers. In Wanzo's words, "[i]llegibility is not invisibility—the victims of Hurricane Katrina and state neglect were hypervisible on television. To be politically illegible as a sufferer is to have one's story visible but obscured by historical and cultural debris, thus the intended audience cannot read or interpret it in a way that leads to true comprehension of the cause of suffering" (32).

6. According to Bernie Cook, Lessin and Deal "used a little more than sixteen minutes of Roberts's footage in *Trouble the Water*, about 17 percent of the film's total running time of ninety-three minutes" (2015:187).

7. This assumption is supported by the film's often-quoted tag line: "It's not about a hurricane. It's about America."

8. First responders and other rescue organizations left a spray painted "X" on the exterior of any building they entered, along with the date of entry, the acronym for their organization, and the number of bodies (dead or living) found inside.

9. These issues are evident in the signs displayed by protesters in the film, and I attended this protest in 2006. See Whitehall and Johnson, who describe scenes such as this one, which offers minimal context regarding the politics of the protest, as obscuring "the lineaments of power shaping this disaster and the process of recovery" (2011:62).

10. A second line is a musical and dance tradition stemming from funeral customs of African Americans in New Orleans: "Traditionally, the jazz musicians and mourners at funerals who were the official part of a procession were the 'first line,' and the people who followed along or beside the official processions were called the 'second line.' People join in unofficially to strut, dance, and improvise their way along the route in New Orleans jazz funerals, Mardi Gras parades, wedding marches, and other processional events.... [A] second line parade—led by a brass band followed by people carrying umbrellas and waving white handkerchiefs—can also be an event in itself" (Ancelet, Gaudet, and Lindahl 2013:xv).

11. As Kim's cousin puts it at one point in the film, "when the storm blew in, it blew away our citizenship."

Chapter Five: Not Written in Stone: Tenth-Anniversary Commemorations of Katrina

1. See Noyes (2016) for a brief discussion of this campaign, as well as useful theorization of "resilience" as what she terms a "slogan-concept."

2. As the Katrina 10 website explains, New Orleans is part of a "100 Resilient Cities" effort supported by the Rockefeller Foundation, which provides funding for cities to develop "resilience strategies" in the face of the "physical, social and economic challenges that are a growing part of the 21st century" (see http://www.100resilientcities.org/about-us#/-_/).

3. Charity, one of the country's longest-operating public hospitals, was closed in the wake of Katrina, despite objections and controversy (see, for example, Gratz 2011).

4. As Lindsay Tuggle describes it, "The Katrina Memorial engraves its labyrinthine hurricane over thousands of anonymous graves, displacing the casualties of generational poverty with a monument to disaster" (2015:135).

5. Coroners are elected officials in New Orleans. Rouse was elected in 2014, replacing Minyard, who had been coroner since 1973. While under Minyard's leadership, the coroner's office had been criticized for its role in classifying deaths occurring in police custody, with allegations that it protected police by classifying deaths as accidental or undetermined rather than homicide. Though Rouse had worked under Minyard before running to replace him, he campaigned on the platform that he would bring reforms, and he has taken steps toward greater transparency since his election, making him a relatively popular public figure (Maggi 2011; Bishop and Sale 2015).

6. The Road Home program, funded by the Department of Housing and Urban Development, has been beleaguered since its inception after Katrina and widely subject to criticism (see for example Hammer 2015).

7. "Ashe" (also spelled "áshe or "ase") is a Yoruba concept with sacred, secular, and aesthetic meanings in Africa and in the African diaspora. In the United States, for example, it

might refer to spiritual power in a religious context or other kinds of power in secular discourse. Robert Farris Thompson explains that "*áshe* literally means 'So be it,' 'May it happen'" (1983:7), which is the sense in which it was used during this New Orleans ceremony.

8. Melanie Deffendall has faced her own difficult recovery, some of which she detailed in a 2006 interview with her son described in the *Baton Rouge Advocate* (Guarino 2015).

9. Attendees primarily came out of an interest to learn the skills being taught, and some expressed a desire to share their stories or hear the stories of others. In true college campus fashion, I also offered free pizza as an incentive to participate.

10. Will Bercik, e-mail message to author, August 27, 2015.

Conclusion

1. New Orleans Police officers were convicted of shooting unarmed civilians as they tried to evacuate the city—killing two people—and then covering up the evidence. The officers were not sentenced until 2016; see for example Daley and Lane (2016).

2. For an insightful analysis of intersections between Katrina and sports commentary, see Serazio (2010). Serazio writes regarding coverage of the New Orleans Saints' 2006 football season, "a largely uniform media narrative emerged—one which relentlessly employed a winning team as the trope for metaphorical recovery. . . . For the nation, a feel-good, comeback story from New Orleans could absolve guilt over the tragedy and its neglected aftermath" (156).

3. Although it is tangential here, there is much more of interest that can be and in fact has been said about "Formation"; see for example Arzumanova (2016); Doubek (2016); Lewis (2016).

4. For scholarly discussion of such initiatives in New Orleans, see, for example, Morgan, Morgan, and Barrett (2006), on historic preservation, and Brown (2015), on African American youth mentoring programs.

5. Rose offers this definition in the context of discussing how critics interpret visual texts; she critiques their tendency to assume their interpretation is universal (2001).

6. Katherine Borland (1991) also makes a persuasive case for dialogic ethnographic writing. Like Lawless, Borland focuses primarily on the product of interview-based research, rather than its processes.

7. I have written elsewhere in greater detail about the dual roles of survivor and scholar, discussing my relative privilege in experiencing Katrina and the special insights that survivor-ethnographers can offer (Horigan 2017).

8. For more on the problems and possibilities inherent in disaster tourism in New Orleans, see Pezzullo (2009).

9. See for example http://louisianamusichalloffame.org/content/view/35/72/.

10. See for example Tierney, Bevc, and Kuligowski (2006); Solnit (2009); Lindahl (2013).

BIBLIOGRAPHY

Abrahams, Roger D., with Nick Spitzer, John F. Szwed, and Robert Farris Thompson. 2006. *Blues for New Orleans: Mardi Gras and America's Creole Soul.* Philadelphia: University of Pennsylvania Press.

Albert_F. 2012. Comment on Schwiegershausen, Erica. "Protagonist of Dave Eggers's 'Zeitoun' Arrested Again." *The New York Observer.* August 7 (comments since removed), http://observer.com/2012/08/ protagonist-of-dave-eggerss-zeitoun-arrested-again/.

Ancelet, Barry Jean, Marcia Gaudet, and Carl Lindahl, eds. 2013. *Second Line Rescue: Improvised Responses to Katrina and Rita.* Jackson: University Press of Mississippi.

Arzumanova, Inna. 2016. "The Culture Industry and Beyoncé's Proprietary Blackness." *Celebrity Studies* 7 (3): 421–24.

Assmann, Aleida. 2006. "History, Memory, and the Genre of Testimony." *Poetics Today* 27 (2): 261–73.

Bal, Mieke, Jonathon Crewe, and Leo Spitzer, eds. 1999. *Acts of Memory: Cultural Recall in the Present.* Hanover, NH: University Press of New England.

"Barbara Bush Calls Evacuees Better Off." *The New York Times,* September 7, 2005.

Barrios, Roberto E. 2014. "'Here, I'm Not at Ease': Anthropological Perspectives on Community Resilience." *Disasters* 38 (2): 329–50.

Barry, John. 1997. *Rising Tide: The Great Mississippi Flood of 1927 and How It Changed America.* New York: Simon & Schuster.

Bauman, Richard. 1975. "Verbal Art as Performance." *American Anthropologist* 77 (2): 290–311.

———. 1986. *Story, Performance, and Event: Contextual Study of Oral Narrative.* Cambridge: Cambridge University Press.

———. 1992. "Performance." In *Folklore, Cultural Performances, and Popular Entertainments,* edited by Richard Bauman, 41–49. Oxford: Oxford University Press.

Beiner, Guy. 2007. *Remembering the Year of the French: Irish Folk History and Social Memory.* Madison: University of Wisconsin Press.

Ben-Amos, Dan. 1971. "Toward a Definition of Folklore in Context." *Journal of American Folklore* 84 (331): 3–15.

Berlant, Lauren, ed. 2004. *Compassion: The Culture and Politics of an Emotion.* New York: Routledge.

Beverley, John. 2004. *Testimonio: On the Politics of Truth.* Minneapolis: University of Minnesota Press.

Biehl, João. 2005. *Vita: Life in a Zone of Social Abandonment*. Berkeley: University of California Press.

Bishop, Katie, and Anna Sale. 2015. "How Katrina Turned a Psychiatrist into a Coroner." *The Atlantic*, August 25.

Bock, Sheila, and Kate Parker Horigan. 2015. "Invoking the Relative: A New Perspective on Family Lore in Stigmatized Communities." *Diagnosing Folklore: Perspectives on Health, Trauma, and Disability*, edited by Trevor J. Blank and Andrea Kitta, 65–84. Jackson: University Press of Mississippi.

Bohmer, Carol, and Amy Shuman. 2008. *Rejecting Refugees: Political Asylum in the 21st Century*. New York: Routledge.

Borland, Katherine. 1991. "'That's Not What I Said': Interpretive Conflict in Oral Narrative Research." In *Women's Words: The Feminist Practice of Oral History*, edited by Sherna Berger Gluck and Daphne Patai, 63–76. New York: Routledge.

Briggs, Charles. 1986. *Learning How to Ask: A Sociolinguistic Appraisal of the Role of the Interview in Social Science Research*. Cambridge: Cambridge University Press.

———. 1988. *Competence in Performance: The Creativity of Tradition in Mexicano Verbal Art*. Philadelphia: University of Pennsylvania Press.

———. 2005. "Communicability, Racial Discourse, and Disease." *Annual Review of Anthropology* 34: 269–91.

Brown, Nikki. 2015. "In the Wake of the Storm: Mentoring Programs, Community Groups, and a New Civil Rights Movement after Hurricane Katrina." *Black Scholar* 45 (3): 10–23.

Brown, Robbie. 2012. "Katrina Hero Facing Charges in New Orleans." *The New York Times*, August 9.

Brummett, Barry. 1991. *Rhetorical Dimensions of Popular Culture*. Tuscaloosa: University of Alabama Press.

Caplan, Eric Michael. 1995. "Trains, Brains, and Sprains: Railway Spine and the Origins of Psychoneuroses." *Bulletin of the History of Medicine* 69 (3): 387–419.

Cashman, Ray. 2008. *Storytelling on the Northern Irish Border: Characters and Community*. Bloomington: Indiana University Press.

———. 2012. "Situational Context and Interaction in a Folklorist's Ethnographic Approach to Storytelling." In *Varieties of Narrative Analysis*, edited by James A. Holstein and Jaber F. Gubrium, 181–204. Thousand Oaks, CA: SAGE.

Chan, Christian S., Jean E. Rhodes, and John E. Pérez. 2012. "A Prospective Study of Religiousness and Psychological Distress among Female Survivors of Hurricanes Katrina and Rita." *American Journal of Community Psychology* 49: 168–81.

Chute, Hillary. 2008. "Comics as Literature? Reading Graphic Narrative." *PMLA* 123 (2): 452–65.

Clarkson, Jacquelyn, and Arnie Fielkow. Adopted August 2010. "Plan for the 21st Century: New Orleans 2030." New Orleans City Council Ordinance #24,079 M.C.S. Web. 16 February 2013, http://www.nola.gov.

Classen, Constance, David Howes, and Anthony Synnott. 1994. *Aroma: The Cultural History of Smell*. London: Routledge.

Coates, Jennifer. 2007. "Talk in a Play Frame: More on Laughter and Intimacy." *Journal of Pragmatics* 39: 29–49.

Coby, Jim. 2015. "'—It's Pretty Easy to Forget What It's Like to Be a Have-Not': Envisioning and Experiencing Trauma in Josh Neufeld's *A.D.: New Orleans after the Deluge*." *South Central Review* 32 (3): 110–23.

Collins, Patricia Hill. 1986. "Learning from the Outsider Within: The Sociological Significance of Black Feminist Thought." In "Special Theory Issue." *Social Problems* 33 (6): S14–S32.

Colten, Craig E., and Alexandra Giancarlo. 2011. "Losing Resilience on the Gulf Coast: Hurricanes and Social Memory." *Environment: Science and Policy for Sustainable Development* 53 (4): 6–18.

Comic Book News and Reviews: Pulp Secret Report. May 15, 2007. YouTube video, 4:58, http://www.youtube.com/watch?v=kdMpxlgEoic.

Cook, Bernie. 2015. *Flood of Images: Media, Memory, and Hurricane Katrina*. Austin: University of Texas Press.

Cook, Stephen W., Jamie D. Aten, Michael Moore, Joshua N. Hook, and Don E. Davis. 2013. "Resource Loss, Religiousness, Health, and Posttraumatic Growth Following Hurricane Katrina." *Mental Health, Religion & Culture* 16 (4): 352–66.

Cortazzi, Martin. 2001. "Narrative Analysis in Ethnography." In *Handbook of Ethnography*, edited by Paul Atkinson, Amanda Coffey, Sara Delamont, John Lofland, and Lyn Lofland. London: SAGE.

Crenshaw, Kimberle. 1991. "Mapping the Margins: Intersectionality, Identity Politics, and Violence against Women of Color." *Stanford Law Review* 43 (July): 1241–99.

Dahmen, Nicole Smith, and Andrea Miller. 2012. "Redefining Iconicity: A Five-Year Study of Visual Themes of Hurricane Katrina." *Visual Communication Quarterly* 19 (1): 4–19.

Daley, Ken, and Emily Lane. 2016. "Danziger Bridge Officers Sentenced: 7–12 Years for Shooters, Cop in Cover-up Gets 3." *The Times-Picayune*, April 20.

de Caro, Frank. 2013. *Stories of Our Lives: Memory, History, Narrative*. Logan: Utah State University Press.

de Certeau, Michel. 1984. *The Practice of Everyday Life*. Translated by Steven F. Rendall. Berkeley: University of California Press.

de Lauretis, Teresa. 1984. *Alice Doesn't: Feminism, Semiotics, Cinema*. Bloomington: Indiana University Press.

Dickinson, Greg, Carole Blair, and Brian L. Ott, eds. 2010. *Places of Public Memory: The Rhetoric of Museums and Memorials*. Tuscaloosa: University of Alabama Press.

Donica, Joseph. 2015. "Disaster's Ethics of Literature: Voicing Katrina's Stories in a Digital Age." In *Ten Years after Katrina: Critical Perspectives of the Storm's Effect on American Culture and Identity*, edited by Mary Ruth Marotte and Glenn Jellenik, 3–16. Lanham, MD: Lexington Books.

Doubek, James. 2016. "With 'Formation,' Beyoncé Lights Up the Internet. Here's What People Are Saying." *All Things Considered*. National Public Radio, February 7.

Doughty, Ruth. 2012. "Katrina's City? New Orleans, Race, Myth, Forced Migration and Return." *Crossings: Journal of Migration and Culture* 3 (2): 255–70.

Dundes, Alan. 1980. *Interpreting Folklore*. Bloomington: Indiana University Press.

Duranti, Alessandro, and Charles Goodwin. 1992. *Rethinking Context: Language as an Interactive Phenomenon*. Cambridge: Cambridge University Press.

Egan, Timothy. 2009. "After the Deluge." Review of *Zeitoun*, by Dave Eggers. *The New York Times*, August 16.

Eggers, Dave. 2009a. "War on Terror, Katrina Intersect in *Zeitoun*." Interview with Guy Raz. *All Things Considered*. National Public Radio, July 25.

———. 2009b. *Zeitoun*. San Francisco: McSweeney's Books.

Elliot, Jane. 2010. "Life Preservers: The Neoliberal Enterprise of Hurricane Katrina Survival in *Trouble the Water, House M.D.*, and *When the Levees Broke*." In *Old and New Media after Katrina*, edited by Diane Negra, 89–112. New York: Palgrave Macmillan.

Erikson, Kai. 1994. *A New Species of Trouble: The Human Experience of Modern Disasters.* New York: W. W. Norton.

Erikson, Kai, and Lori Peek. 2011. *Hurricane Katrina Research Bibliography*. Social Science Research Council, Task Force on Katrina and Rebuilding the Gulf Coast.

Eyerman, Ron. 2015. *Is This America? Katrina as Cultural Trauma*. Austin: University of Texas Press.

Fairclough, Norman. 1995. *Critical Discourse Analysis: The Critical Study of Language*. Essex: Longman Group.

Fassin, Didier, and Richard Rechtman. 2009. *Empire of Trauma: An Inquiry into the Condition of Victimhood*. Translated by Rachel Gomme. Princeton, NJ: Princeton University Press.

Felman, Shoshana, and Dori Laub. 1992. *Testimony: Crises of Witnessing in Literature, Psychoanalysis, and History*. New York: Routledge.

Frank, Arthur. 1995. *The Wounded Storyteller: Body, Illness, and Ethics*. Chicago: University of Chicago Press.

Gaines, Kevin K. 1996. *Uplifting the Race: Black Leadership, Politics, and Culture in the Twentieth Century*. Chapel Hill: University of North Carolina Press.

Galofaro, Claire. 2013. "Celebrated Hurricane Katrina Protagonist Zeitoun Facing Additional Charge." *The Times-Picayune*, March 8.

Garfield, Gail. 2007. "Hurricane Katrina: The Making of Unworthy Disaster Victims." *Journal of African American Studies* 10 (4): 55–74.

Gaudet, Marcia. 2013. "'Don't Get Stuck on Stupid': General Honoré as Culture Hero." In *Second Line Rescue: Improvised Responses to Katrina and Rita*, edited by Barry Jean Ancelet, Marcia Gaudet, and Carl Lindahl, 62–72. Jackson: University Press of Mississippi.

Gentilviso, Chris. 2013. "Michael Brown Superdome Comment: Ex-FEMA Director Sparks Super Bowl Blackout Controversy." *Thehuffingtonpost.com*, February 4.

Gibson, Timothy. 2006. "New Orleans and the Wisdom of Lived Space." *Space and Culture* 9 (1): 45–47.

Gilmore, Leigh. 2001. *The Limits of Autobiography: Trauma and Testimony*. Ithaca: Cornell University Press.

Gipson, Jennifer. 2014. "Lafcadio Hearn, Hurricane Katrina, and Mardi Gras: A Nineteenth-Century Folklorist's New Life in New Orleans." *Western Folklore* 73 (2/3): 173–94.

Goffman, Erving. 1959. *The Presentation of Self in Everyday Life*. New York: Doubleday.

Goldstein, Diane. 2015. "Vernacular Turns: Narrative, Local Knowledge, and the Changed Context of Folklore." *Journal of American Folklore* 128 (508): 125–45.

Goodall, Jane, and Christopher Lee. 2015. "Introduction." In *Trauma and Public Memory*, edited by Jane Goodall and Christopher Lee, 1–20. Hampshire: Palgrave Macmillan.

Gratz, Roberta Brandes. 2011. "Why Was New Orleans's Charity Hospital Allowed to Die?" *The Nation*, April 27.

Grimm, Andy. 2015. "For Some, Katrina's Anniversary Can't Pass Soon Enough." *The Times-Picayune*, August 29.

Guarino, Mark. 2015. "Delgado Instructor Tells Son of Struggle to Reclaim Her Old Life after Storm." *The Baton Rouge Advocate*, August 23.

Gubrium, Jaber F., and James A. Holstein. 2009. *Analyzing Narrative Reality*. Thousand Oaks, CA: SAGE.

Halbwachs, Maurice. 1992. *On Collective Memory*. Translated by Lewis A. Coser. Chicago: University of Chicago Press.

Hammer, David. 2015. "Examining Post-Katrina Road Home Program." *The Baton Rouge Advocate*, August 23.

Hartnell, Anna. 2010. "Katrina Tourism and a Tale of Two Cities: Visualizing Race and Class in New Orleans." In *In the Wake of Hurricane Katrina: New Paradigms and Social Visions*, edited by Clyde Woods, 297–321. Baltimore: Johns Hopkins University Press.

Haskins, Ekaterina V. 2015. *Popular Memories: Commemoration, Participatory Culture, and Democratic Citizenship*. Columbia: University of South Carolina Press.

Heitger, Raymond Albert. 2005. "Thermal Infrared Imaging for the Charity Hospital Cemetery Archaeological Survey." MA Thesis, University of New Orleans.

Hesford, Wendy S. 2011. *Spectacular Rhetorics: Human Rights Visions, Recognitions, Feminisms*. Durham: Duke University Press.

Hill, Jane H., and Ofelia Zepeda. 1993. "Mrs. Patricio's Trouble: The Distribution of Responsibility in an Account of Personal Experience." In *Responsibility and Evidence in Oral Discourse*, edited by Jane Hill and Judith T. Irvine, 197–225. New York: Cambridge University Press.

Hirsch, Arnold R., and A. Lee Levert. 2009. "The Katrina Conspiracies: The Problem of Trust in Rebuilding an American City." *Journal of Urban History* 35 (2): 207–19.

Hirsch, Marianne. 2004. "Editor's Column: Collateral Damage." *PMLA* 119 (5): 1209–15.

Hoefer, Anthony Dyer. 2012. "A Re-Vision of the Record: The Demands of Reading Josh Neufeld's *A.D.: New Orleans after the Deluge*." In *Comics and the U.S. South*, edited by Brannon Costello and Qiana J. Whitted, 293–323. Jackson: University of Mississippi Press.

Hoeschmann, Michael, and Bronwen E. Low. 2008. *Reading Youth Writing: "New" Literacies, Cultural Studies and Education*. New York: Peter Lang.

Holstein, James A., and Jaber F. Gubrium. 2004. "Context: Working It Up, Down, and Across." In *Qualitative Research Practice*, edited by Clive Seale, Giampietro Gobo, Jaber F. Gubrium, and David Silverman, 267–81. London: SAGE.

Horigan, Kate Parker. 2017. "Critical Empathy: A Survivor's Study of Disaster." *Fabula* 58 (1–2): 76–89.

"Hurricane Katrina Memorial." *Stull and Lee Incorporated*. Accessed August 9, 2016. http://stullandlee.com/architecture/hurricane-katrina-memorial/.

Hymes, Dell. 1974. *Foundations in Sociolinguistics: An Ethnographic Approach*. Philadelphia: University of Pennsylvania Press.

Kaplan, Ann. 2005. *Trauma Culture: The Politics of Terror and Loss in Media and Literature*. New Brunswick, NJ: Rutgers University Press.

Keeble, A. G. 2014. "Katrina Time: An Aggregation of Political Rhetoric in *Zeitoun*." In *Ten Years after Katrina: Critical Perspectives of the Storm's Effect on American Culture and Identity*, edited by Mary Ruth Marotte and Glenn Jellenik. Lanham, MD: Lexington Books.

Kelman, Ari. 2009. "Even Paranoids Have Enemies: Rumors of Levee Sabotage in New Orleans's Lower Ninth Ward." *Journal of Urban History* 35 (5): 627–39.

Klapp, Orrin E. 1949. "The Folk Hero." *Journal of American Folklore* 62 (243): 17–25.

Kleinschrodt, Michael. 2015. "Hurricane Katrina 10th Anniversary Events: A Complete Guide to August 29." *NOLA.com*.

Kverndokk, Kyrre. 2014. "Mediating the Morals of Disasters: Hurricane Katrina in Norwegian News Media." *Nordic Journal of Science and Technology Studies* 2 (1): 78–87.

Labov, William. 1982. "Speech Actions and Reactions in Personal Narrative." In *Georgetown University Round Table on Languages and Linguistics 1981: Text and Talk*, edited by Deborah Tannen, 219–47. Washington, DC: Georgetown University Press.

Labov, William, and Joshua Waletzky. 1967. "Narrative Analysis: Oral Versions of Personal Experience." In *Essays on the Verbal and Visual Arts: Proceedings of the 1966 Annual Spring Meeting of the American Ethnological Society*, edited by June Helm, 12–44. Seattle: University of Washington Press.

LaCapra, Dominick. 2001. *Writing History, Writing Trauma*. Baltimore: Johns Hopkins University Press.

Lawless, Elaine. 1992. "'I Was Afraid Someone Like You . . . an Outsider . . . Would Misunderstand': Negotiating Interpretive Differences between Ethnographers and Subjects." *The Journal of American Folklore* 105 (417): 302–14.

Lawrence, David Todd. 2015. "The Rural Black Nowhere: Invisibility, Urbannormativity, and the Geography of Indifference." *The Journal of the Midwest Modern Language Association* 48 (1): 221–44.

Lessin, Tia, and Carl Deal. Interview. *HBO.com*. Home Box Office, n.d. Accessed September 4, 2012, http://www.hbo.com/documentaries/trouble-the-water/interview/carl-deal-and -tia-lessin.html.

Lewis, Shantrelle. 2016. "'Formation' Exploits New Orleans' Trauma." *Slate.com*, February 10.

Lindahl, Carl. 2012a. "How Do Survivors Respond to Disasters?" Abstract in *The Continuity and Creativity of Culture: Annual Meeting Program and Abstracts*, 55. Columbus, OH: The American Folklore Society.

———. 2012b. "Legends of Hurricane Katrina: The Right to Be Wrong, Survivor-to-Survivor Storytelling, and Healing." *Journal of American Folklore* 125 (496): 139–76.

———. 2013. "Epilogue: A Street Named Desire." In *Second Line Rescue: Improvised Responses to Katrina and Rita*, edited by Barry Jean Ancelet, Marcia Gaudet, and Carl Lindahl, 248–59. Jackson: University Press of Mississippi.

Linde, Charlotte. 1993. *Life Stories: Creation of Coherence*. Oxford: Oxford University Press.

Lloyd, Christopher. 2014. "Dave Eggers' *Zeitoun* and Katrina's Southern Biopolitics." In *Ten Years after Katrina: Critical Perspectives of the Storm's Effect on American Culture and Identity*, edited by Mary Ruth Marotte and Glenn Jellenik. Lanham, MD: Lexington Books.

Lopez, Kenny. 2013. "'Millionaire's Row': Who Is Buried in Metairie Cemetery?" *WGNO.com*.

MacCash, Doug. 2015. "Katrina 10 Commemorative Second Line Achieves Full Resonance." *The Times-Picayune*, August 29.

Madsen, Wendy, and Cathy O'Mullan. 2013. "Responding to Disaster: Applying the Lens of Social Memory." *Australian Journal of Communication* 40 (1): 57–70.

Maggi, Laura. 2011. "Orleans Parish Coroner's Office Autopsies of Some Who Died in Police Custody Are Questioned." *The Times-Picayune*, January 30.

Martin, Naomi. 2013. "Zeitoun Found Not Guilty on Charges He Tried to Kill His Ex-wife." *The Times-Picayune*, July 30.

McCarthy, Brendan. 2012. "Judge Imposes Stiff Sentences on 5 NOPD Officers Convicted in Danziger Shootings." *The Times-Picayune*, April 4.

McCloud, Scott. 1993. *Understanding Comics: The Invisible Art*. New York: HarperPerennial.

———. 2005. "The Visual Magic of Comics." TED video, 17:08. Ted.com.

McWhirter, Cameron. 2015. "New Orleans Honors Katrina's Victims on Storm's 10th Anniversary." *The Wall Street Journal*, August 29.

Mechling, Jay. 1998. "Heroism and the Problem of Impulsiveness for Early Twentieth-Century American Youth." In *Generations of Youth: Youth Cultures and History in Twentieth-Century America*, edited by Joe Austin and Michael Nevin Willard. New York: New York University Press.

———. 2004. "Picturing Hunting." *Western Folklore* 63 (1/2): 51–78.

Morgan, David W., Nancy I. M. Morgan, and Brenda Barrett. 2006. "Finding a Place for the Commonplace: Hurricane Katrina, Communities, and Preservation Law." *American Anthropologist* 108 (4): 706–18.

Morris, Benjamin. 2009. "Hurricane Katrina and the Arts of Remembrance." In *Moment to Monument: The Making and Unmaking of Cultural Significance*, edited by Ladina Bezzola Lambert and Andrea Ochsner, 155–68. New Brunswick, NJ: Transaction.

Mustian, Jim. 2015. "Despite Enormity of Disaster, New Orleans Region Lacks Definitive Katrina Memorial." *The New Orleans Advocate*, August 29.

Myerhoff, Barbara. 1992. *Remembered Lives: The Work of Ritual, Storytelling, and Growing Older*. Edited by Marc Kaminsky. Ann Arbor: University of Michigan Press.

Negra, Diane. 2010. *Old and New Media after Katrina*. New York: Palgrave Macmillan.

Neufeld, Josh. 2007–8. *A.D.: New Orleans after the Deluge*. SMITH Magazine, http://www.smithmag.net/afterthedeluge/2007/01/01/prologue-1/.

———. 2009a. *A.D.: New Orleans after the Deluge*. New York: Pantheon.

———. 2009b. "A Short Interview with Josh Neufeld." By Tom Spurgeon. *The Comics Reporter*, August 19.

———. 2009c. "*A.D.: New Orleans after the Deluge*: Josh Neufeld Q&A." By Noah Bonaparte Pais. *Gambit Weekly*, August 20.

———. 2016. "My Intro to Creating Comics as Journalism, Memoir & Nonfiction," February 5, https://joshcomix.wordpress.com/2016/02/05/my-intro-to-creating-comics-as-journalismmemoir-nonfiction/.

Noyes, Dorothy. 2016. *Humble Theory: Folklore's Grasp on Social Life*. Bloomington: Indiana University Press.

Ó Ciosáin, Niall. 2004. "Approaching a Folklore Archive: The Irish Folklore Commission and the Memory of the Great Famine." *Folklore* 115 (2): 222–32.

Olick, Jeffrey K., and Joyce Robbins. 1998. "Social Memory Studies: From 'Collective Memory' to the Historical Sociology of Mnemonic Practices." *Annual Review of Sociology* 24: 105–40.

Oliver, Kelly. 2001. *Witnessing: Beyond Recognition*. Minneapolis: University of Minnesota Press.

Olney, James. 1984. "A Theory of Autobiography." In *Autobiography: Essays Theoretical and Critical*, edited by James Olney. Princeton, NJ: Princeton University Press.

Oswald, Stephanie. 2015. "Cemetery Invites Public to Participate in Unique Katrina Memorial." *WGNO.com*.

Palmenfelt, Ulf. 2011. "The Celestial Attraction of the Invisible Grand Narratives." Lecture given at Ohio State University, Columbus, OH, October 17.

Paredes, Américo. 1964. "Some Aspects of Folk Poetry." *Texas Studies in Literature and Language* 6 (2): 213–25.

Patrice. 2006a. Interview by Adele. Houston, Texas, January 2006. SKRH Database.

———. 2006b. Interview by Sheryl. Houston, Texas, November 2006. SKRH Database.

Patterson, Victoria. 2012. "Did Dave Eggers Get 'Zeitoun' Wrong?" *Salon*, December 9.

Pezzullo, Phaedra C. 2009. "Tourists and/as Disasters: Rebuilding, Remembering, and Responsibility in New Orleans." *Tourist Studies* 9 (1): 23–41.

Phillips, Kendall R., ed. 2004. *Framing Public Memory*. Tuscaloosa: University of Alabama Press.

Pintar, Judith. 2006. "Rethinking Trauma in the Hurricane's Wake." *Space and Culture* 9 (1): 52–54.

Plummer, Ken. 2001. "The Call of Life Stories in Ethnographic Research." In *Handbook of Ethnography*, edited by Paul Atkinson, Amanda Coffey, Sara Delamont, John Lofland, and Lyn Lofland, 395–406. London: SAGE.

Portelli, Alessandro. 1991. *The Death of Luigi Trastulli, and Other Stories: Form and Meaning in Oral History*. Albany: State University of New York Press.

"Post-Katrina Depicted in Comic Strips." 2007. *News and Notes*, interview by Farai Chideya. National Public Radio, August 24.

Roberts, John W. 1990. *From Trickster to Badman: The Black Folk Hero in Slavery and Freedom*. Philadelphia: University of Pennsylvania Press.

Rose, Gillian. 2001. *Visual Methodologies: An Introduction to the Interpretation of Visual Materials*. London: SAGE.

Ross, Marlon B. 2007. "Introduction." *Let Me Live*, by Angelo Herndon. Ann Arbor: University of Michigan Press.

Rothberg, Michael. 2009. *Multidirectional Memory: Remembering the Holocaust in the Age of Decolonization*. Stanford: Stanford University Press.

Rowell, Charles Henry, ed. 2006. "American Tragedy: New Orleans under Water." Special issue, *Callaloo* 29 (4).

Sánchez-Carretero, Cristina. 2011. "The Madrid Train Bombings: Enacting the Emotional Body at the March 11 Grassroots Memorials." In *Grassroots Memorials: The Politics of Memorializing Traumatic Death*, edited by Peter Jan Margry and Cristina Sánchez-Carretero, 244–61. New York: Berghahn Books.

Sawin, Patricia. 2004. *Listening for a Life: A Dialogic Ethnography of Bessy Eldreth through Her Songs*. Logan: Utah State University Press.

Schaffer, Kay, and Sidonie Smith. 2004. *Human Rights and Narrated Lives: The Ethics of Recognition*. New York: Palgrave MacMillan.

Schiffrin, Deborah, Deborah Tannen, and Heidi E. Hamilton, eds. 2008. *The Handbook of Discourse Analysis*. Malden, MA: Blackwell.

Schwartz, Gretchen. 2010. "Graphic Novels, New Literacies, and Good Old Social Justice." *The ALAN Review* 37 (3): 71–75.

Scott, Joan W. 1991. "The Evidence of Experience." *Critical Inquiry* 17 (4): 773–97.

Selzer, Linda. 2009. "Instruments More Perfect than Bodies: Romancing Uplift in Colson Whitehead's *The Intuitionist*." *African American Review* 43 (4): 681–98.

Serazio, Michael. 2010. "When the Sportswriters Go Marching In: Sports Journalism, Collective Trauma, and Memory Metaphors." *Critical Studies in Media Communication* 27 (2): 155–73.

Seremetakis, C. Nadia. 1993. "The Memory of the Senses: Historical Perception, Commensal Exchange and Modernity." *Visual Anthropology Review* 9: 2–18.

Shawn. 2008. Interview by Amber. Houston, Texas, June 2008. SKRH Database.

Shuman, Amy. 2005. *Other People's Stories: Entitlement Claims and the Critique of Empathy*. Champaign: University of Illinois Press.

Siepmann, Philipp. 2015. "Natural Hazards, Human Vulnerability: Teaching Hurricane Katrina through Literary Nonfiction." In *After the Storm: The Cultural Politics of Hurricane Katrina*, edited by Simon Dickel and Evangelia Kindinger, 131–45. Beilefeld, Germany: Transcript Verlag.

Simerman, John. 2014. "Abdulrahman Zeitoun, Once Literary Hero, Returns to Court in Jail Garb." *The New Orleans Advocate*, May 23.

SKRH [Surviving Katrina and Rita in Houston]. 2006–. Database. Containing information on 433 audio-recorded narratives in FileMaker Pro 8.5 format. Houston Folklore Archive, University of Houston, Houston, TX.

Solnit, Rebecca. 2009. *A Paradise Built in Hell: The Extraordinary Communities That Arise in Disaster*. New York: Penguin Books.

Sothern, Billy. 2007. *Down in New Orleans: Reflections from a Drowned City*. Oakland: University of California Press.

Stahl, Sandra K. D. 1989. *Literary Folkloristics and the Personal Narrative*. Bloomington: Indiana University Press.

Stein, Alan H., and Gene B. Preuss. 2008. "Oral History, Folklore, and Katrina." *Louisiana Folklore Miscellany* 16–17: 98–122.

Stein, Letitia. 2015. "Katrina's Unclaimed Dead Conjure Memories of Her Ravages." *Reuters. com*, August 25.

Stevens, Maurice. 2006. "From the Deluge: Traumatic Iconography and Emergent Visions of Nation in Katrina's Wake." *English Language Notes* 44 (2): 217–25.

———. 2009. "From the Past Imperfect: Towards a Critical Trauma Theory." *Letters: The Semiannual Newsletter of the Robert Penn Warren Center for the Humanities* 17 (2): 1–5.

"Surviving Katrina and Rita in Houston." 2010. *Houston History Magazine* 7 (3): 37–40.

Sutton, David E. 2001. *Remembrance of Repasts: An Anthropology of Food and Memory*. New York: Berg.

Thibodeau, Ruth. 1989. "From Racism to Tokenism: The Changing Face of Blacks in *New Yorker* Cartoons." *Public Opinion Quarterly* 53 (4): 482–94.

Thomas, Lynnell L. 2014. *Desire & Disaster in New Orleans*. Durham: Duke University Press.

Thomas, Valorie. 2012. "'Dust to Cleanse Themselves,' A Survivor's Ethos: Diasporic Disidentifications in *Zeitoun*." *Biography* 35 (2): 271–85.

Thompson, Robert Farris. 1984. *Flash of the Spirit: African and Afro-American Art and Philosophy*. New York: Vintage.

Tierney, Kathleen, Christine Bevc, and Erica Kuligowski. 2006. "Metaphors Matter: Disaster Myths, Media Frames, and Their Consequences in Hurricane Katrina." *Annals of the American Academy of Political and Social Science* 604 (1): 57–81.

Titon, Jeff Todd. 1980. "The Life Story." *Journal of American Folklore* 93 (369): 276–92.

Tonkin, Elizabeth. 1992. *Narrating Our Pasts: The Social Construction of Oral History*. Cambridge: Cambridge University Press.

Trouble the Water. Directed by Tia Lessen and Carl Deal. 2008. Perf. Kimberly Roberts, Scott Roberts. Elsewhere Films. DVD.

Tuggle, Lindsay. 2015. "Unburied Trauma and the Exhumation of History: An American Genealogy." In *Trauma and Public Memory*, edited by Jane Goodall and Christopher Lee, 131–46. New York: Palgrave MacMillan.

Van Alphen, Ernst. 1997. *Caught by History: Holocaust Effects in Contemporary Art, Literature, and Theory*. Stanford: Stanford University Press.

———. 1999. "Symptoms of Discursivity: Experience, Memory, and Trauma." In *Acts of Memory: Cultural Recall in the Present*, edited by Mieke Bal, Jonathan Crewe, and Leo Spitzer, 24–38. Hanover, NH: University Press of New England.

Vollen, Lola, and Chris Ying, eds. 2006. *Voices from the Storm*. San Francisco: McSweeney's Books.

Walker, Janet. 2011. "Moving Testimonies and the Geography of Suffering: Perils and Fantasies of Belonging after Katrina." In *Interrogating Trauma: Collective Suffering in Global Arts and Media*, edited by Mick Broderick and Antonio Traverso, 47–64. New York: Routledge.

Wanzo, Rebecca. 2009. *The Suffering Will Not Be Televised*. Albany: State University of New York Press.

White, Sylvia E., and Tania Fuentez. 1997. "Analysis of Black Images in Comic Strips, 1915–1995." *Newspaper Research Journal* 18 (1–2): 72–85.

Whitehall, Geoffrey, and Cedric Johnson. 2011. "Making Citizens in Magnaville." In *The Neoliberal Deluge*, edited by Cedric Johnson, 60–84. Minneapolis: University of Minnesota Press.

Whitlock, Gillian. 2006. "Autographics: The Seeing I of Comics." *Modern Fiction Studies* 52 (4): 965–79.

———. 2007. *Soft Weapons: Autobiography in Transit*. Chicago: University of Chicago Press.

Whitlock, Gillian, and Anna Poletti. 2008. "Self-Regarding Art." *Biography* 31 (1): v–xxiii.

Woodward, Alex. 2015. "Memorials and Second Lines in New Orleans Commemorate Katrina's 10th Anniversary." *The Gambit Weekly*, August 29.

Yaeger, Patricia. 2006. "Testimony without Intimacy." *Poetics Today* 27 (2): 399–423.

Young, Allan. 1995. *The Harmony of Illusions: Inventing Post-Traumatic Stress Disorder.* Princeton, NJ: Princeton University Press.

Zeitoun, Abdulrahman. 2005. "Rescue Efforts Lead to Arrest Nightmare for N.O. Businessman." *The Times-Picayune,* November 24.

INDEX